50 Walks
WILDLIFE

Produced by AA Publishing
© Automobile Association Developments Limited 2007
Illustrations © Automobile Association Developments Limited 2007

Published by AA Publishing (a trading name of Automobile
Association Developments Limited, whose registered office is Fanum
House, Basing View, Basingstoke, Hampshire RG21 4EA;
registered number 1878835)

 This product includes mapping data licensed
from Ordnance Survey* with the permission of
the Controller of Her Majesty's Stationery
Office.© Crown copyright 2007. All rights
reserved. Licence number 100021153

ISBN 978-0-7495-5553-5

A03033e

A CIP catalogue record for this book is available
from the British Library.

The contents of this book are believed correct at the time of printing.
Nevertheless, the publishers cannot be held responsible for any errors
or omissions or for changes in the details given in this book or for
the consequences of any reliance on the information it provides. We
have tried to ensure accuracy in this book, but things do change and
we would be grateful if readers would advise us of any inaccuracies
they may encounter.

We have taken all reasonable steps to ensure that these walks are
safe and achievable by walkers with a realistic level of fitness.
However, all outdoor activities involve a degree of risk and the
publishers accept no responsibility for any injuries caused to
readers whilst following these walks. For more advice on walking
safely see opposite.

Some of the walks may appear in other AA publications.

Visit the AA Publishing website at www.theAA.com

Colour reproduction by Keene Group, Andover
Printed in China by Everbest Printing

Walking in Safety

All these walks are suitable for any reasonably fit person, but less experienced walkers should try the easier walks first. Route finding is usually straightforward, but you will find that an Ordnance Survey map is a useful addition to the route maps and descriptions.

Risks

Although each walk here has been researched with a view to minimising the risks to the walkers who follow its route, no walk in the countryside can be considered to be completely free from risk. Walking in the outdoors will always require a degree of common sense and judgement to ensure that it is as safe as possible.

- Be particularly careful on cliff paths and in upland terrain, where the consequences of a slip can be very serious.

- Remember to check tidal conditions before walking on the seashore.

- Some sections of route are by, or cross, busy roads. Take care and remember traffic is a danger even on minor country lanes.

- Be careful around farmyard machinery and livestock, especially if you have children with you.

- Be aware of the consequences of changes in the weather and check the forecast before you set out. Carry spare clothing and a torch if you are walking in the winter months. Remember the weather can change very quickly at any time of the year, and in moorland and heathland areas, mist and fog can make route finding much harder. Don't set out in these conditions unless you are confident of your navigation skills in poor visibility. In summer remember to take account of the heat and sun; wear a hat and carry spare water.

- On walks away from centres of population you should carry a whistle and survival bag. If you do have an accident requiring the emergency services, make a note of your position as accurately as possible and dial 999.

Legend & map

Legend

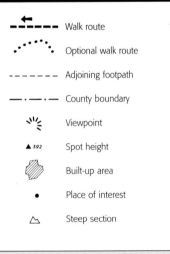

←-------	Walk route	P	Car park
••••••	Optional walk route		Cliff
-------	Adjoining footpath		Rock outcrop
—•—•—	County boundary		Beach
⛰	Viewpoint		Woodland
▲ 392	Spot height		Parkland
	Built-up area	†	Church, cathedral, chapel
•	Place of interest	WC	Toilet
△	Steep section	⊞	Picnic area

locator map

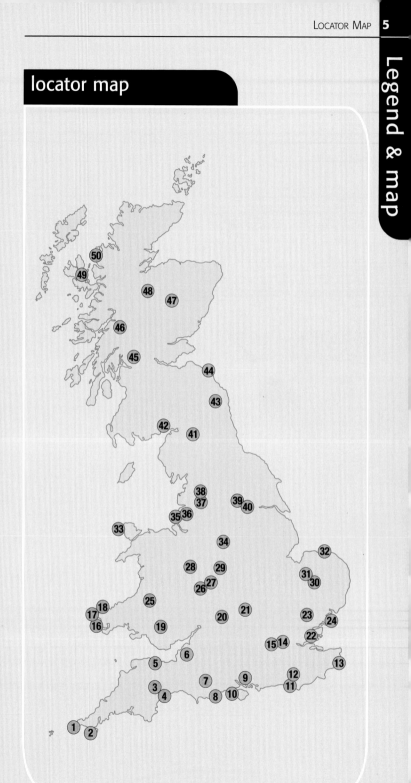

Contents

Contents

Rating: Each walk is rated for its relative difficulty compared to the other walks in this book. Walks marked 🚶🚶🚶 are likely to be shorter and easier with little total ascent. The hardest walks are marked 🚶🚶🚶 .

Walking in Safety: For advice and safety tips see page 3.

Introduction

Encounters with wildlife – whether it be the fleeting glimpse of the disappearing brush of a red squirrel, the melancholy mewing of a bird of prey or the sight of a majestic red deer cantering across a clearing – add enormously to the pleasure of a walk through the British countryside. And with more measures in place than ever before to protect our threatened native habitats – there are now more than 160 National Nature Reserves in England alone and hundreds of Sites of Special Scientific Interest, in addition to the numerous local nature reserves – the chances of having that close encounter with wildlife have never been greater.

The 50 easy-to-follow walks in this book will take you to some of the best – and sometimes most unlikely – places in Britain where, if you are quiet and patient enough, you will see some of the country's best wildlife.

Top of the tree, as it were, is what has been described as Britain's greatest conservation success story – the re-introduction from Norway of the magnificent sea eagle to the Western Isles of Scotland. Walk 49, around Ben Chracaig and Portree Bay on the Isle of Skye, holds out the promise of a possible glimpse of one of these huge birds of prey, which have nested nearby. They can't really be missed because of their huge, eight-foot (2.4m) wingspan, which dwarfs even the mighty golden eagle.

The buzzard – now one of Britain's commonest birds of prey – is often mistaken for a golden eagle in Scotland, where they are sometimes known as 'the tourists' eagle.' One place where you are almost certain to see buzzards (not eagles) is on Walk 3, an easy walk through the National Trust's delightful ancient woodlands flanking the River Dart above Worthy Bridge, west of Tiverton in Devon. This enchanting stroll through Cross's, Huntland and Thongsleigh Woods is enhanced by wild flowers such as bluebells, wood anemones and primroses in the spring.

A good place to study wild flowers is on the Lizard Peninsula in Cornwall, home of the rare Cornish heath which, in late summer, creates a glorious mosaic of colour with its pink and white flowers contrasting with the brilliant yellow of Western gorse and the deeper pinks of cross-leaved heath and bell heather. Walk 2 is a 7-mile (11.3km) stroll through the heart of the Kynance Farm National Nature Reserve, taking in Soap Rock and Gew Graze, or Soapy Cove (both of which are named after the steatite – or soapstone – found there), and the tourist honeypot of Mullion Cove.

The clifftops of the Pembrokeshire Coast are other great places for wild flowers in the spring. Walks 16 (the Marloes Peninsula), 17 (opposite Ramsey Island), and 16 (Strumble Head), have the added bonus of possible sightings of seabirds such as the comical puffin, secretive Manx shearwater and dashing red-billed crow, the chough. And if you are really lucky, you might spot dolphins and harbour porpoises frolicking in the sea below.

Some of our best wildlife habitats are found in the most unlikely places.

Take Sutton Park, 10 miles from the centre of Birmingham, for example. This 2,400 acre (970ha) National Nature Reserve is a charming mixture of heathland, ancient woods and medieval fishponds, circumnavigated in the 7¼ mile (11.7km) walk described in Walk 29. This amazing diversity of habitats earned the park its NNR status in 1997, and it is home to a large number of resident birds as well as being a crucial stop-over for many migrants.

Birders will also love the reserves at Fairburn Ings and Ledsham in West Yorkshire (Walk 40), Martin Mere in Lancashire (Walk 36) and Caerlaverock Castle and the Solway Merses, described in Walk 43, where a large range of wading and waterfowl create a wonderful spectacle, especially during the winter months.

Perhaps the most impressive mammals encountered on these walks are the wild white cattle of Chillingham Park, Northumberland (Walk 42). These magnificent pure white cattle have long sweeping horns and are unrelated to any others in Europe; it is thought that they may be directly descended from the prehistoric auroch. They have lived unmolested in the parkland at Chillingham for 700 years, and can only be approached in the company of an experienced warden.

Using this Book

Information panels
A panel for each walk shows its relative difficulty, the distance and total amount of ascent. An indication of the gradients you will encounter is shown by the rating ▲▲▲ (no steep slopes) to **▲▲▲** (several very steep slopes).

Maps
Each of the 50 walks in this book has its own map, with the walk route clearly marked with a hatched line. Some can be extended by following an extra section of route marked with a dotted line, but for reasons of space, instructions for the extensions are not given in the text. The minimum time suggested for the walk is for reasonably fit walkers and doesn't allow for stops. Each walk has a suggested large-scale OS map which should be used in conjunction with the walk route map. Laminated aqua3 maps are longer lasting and water resistant.

Start Points
The start of each walk is given as a six-figure grid reference prefixed by two letters indicating which 100km square of the National Grid it refers to. You'll find more information on grid references on most Ordnance Survey maps.

Dogs
We have tried to give dog owners useful advice about how dog friendly each walk is. Please respect other countryside users. Keep your dog under control, especially around livestock, and obey local bylaws and other dog control notices.

Car Parking
Many of the car parks suggested are public, but occasionally you may find you have to park on the roadside or in a lay-by. Please be considerate when you leave your car, ensuring that access roads or gates are not blocked and that other vehicles can pass safely.

Golden Beaches and Cliffs at Porthcurno

Along interlocking footpaths between sandy coves and granite cliffs to discover the wildlife of the Land's End Peninsula.

•DISTANCE•	3½ miles (5.7km)
•MINIMUM TIME•	2hrs 30min
•ASCENT / GRADIENT•	164ft (50m) ▲▲▲
•LEVEL OF DIFFICULTY•	🚶 🚶 🚶
•PATHS•	Coastal footpath
•LANDSCAPE•	Granite sea cliffs and inland heath
•SUGGESTED MAP•	aqua3 OS Explorer 107 St Austell & Liskeard
•START / FINISH•	Grid reference: SW 384224
•DOG FRIENDLINESS•	Dogs should be kept under control on beaches
•PARKING•	Porthcurno, St Levan and Porthgwarra
•PUBLIC TOILETS•	Porthgwarra and Porthleven

BACKGROUND TO THE WALK

Land's End may be the ultimate visitor destination in Cornwall. It is the most westerly point certainly and its cliffs are nothing less than spectacular; but for the true aficionado of coastal scenery, the granite cliffs of Porthcurno and Porthgwarra, to the south of Land's End, are hard to beat for their beauty and sculpted form. The area has even more esoteric distinction. Gwennap Head, at Porthgwarra, is the most southerly point on the Land's End Peninsula. The Atlantic tidal flow divides at the base of Gwennap's spectacular Chair Ladder cliff, one flow running eastwards up the English Channel, the other running north, up St George's Channel between Britain and Ireland. Partly because of this, Gwennap Head is sometimes known as 'the Fishermen's Land's End', a title that rather puts the other Land's End in its place.

Golden Sand
This walk starts at Porthcurno, where a sweeping expanse of almost white shell sand lies at the heart of an arc of golden granite cliffs that embrace the small bay. On the south side lies the rocky coxcomb of Treryn Dinas, or Logan Rock. To the north is the famous Minack Open Air Theatre, built within the rocky ribs of the headland. The final section of the walk passes the Minack, but first the route leads inland and across fields to the splendid little Church of St Levan, couched in one of the few sheltered spots on this robust coast. Below the church, a shallow valley runs down to Chapel Porth Beach, more besieged by tides than Porthcurno, but still a delightful place, especially in summer. Again, the beach here is left for later in the walk, whose route now leads along the coastal path and then climbs inland before dropping down to Porthgwarra Cove, where tunnels and caverns in the cliff were carved out by farmers and fishermen to give better access to the narrow beach. From Porthgwarra, you head back along the coastal path to Porth Chapel, (for a visit to Gwennap Head). The path leads you down past the little Well of St Levan. Below here there is a rocky access path to the beach.

Walk 1

Spectacular Steps

The route of the walk leads steeply up to Rospletha Point and then to the remarkable cliff face theatre at Minack (see What to Look For). From here, the most direct way down to Porthcurno Beach is by a series of very steep steps that may not suit everyone. But if you don't mind the vertiginous experience, the views really are outstanding. You can avoid this descent by some judicious road walking. Either way Porthcurno's glorious beach is at hand in the cove below you.

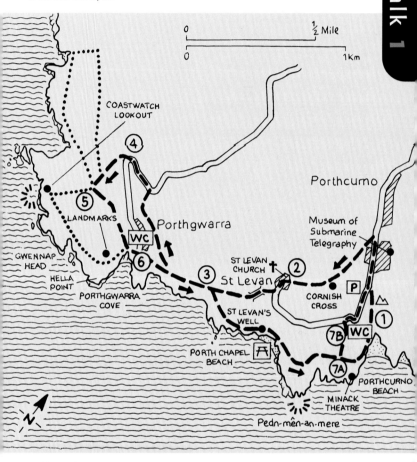

Walk 1 Directions

① From the car park, walk back up the approach road, then just beyond the **Porthcurno Hotel**, turn sharply left along a track and follow it to reach cottages. Pass to the right of the cottages and go through a metal kissing gate. Follow a field path past a granite cross.

② Enter **St Levan** churchyard by a granite stile. Go round the far side of the church to the entrance gate and onto a surfaced lane. Cross the lane and follow the path opposite, signposted 'Porthgwarra Cove'. Cross a footbridge over a stream then in about 55yds (50m), at a junction, take the right fork and follow the path to merge with the main coast path and keep ahead.

③ Just after the path begins to descend towards **Porthgwarra Cove**, branch off right up some wooden steps. Reach a track and turn up right, then at a road, turn left.

④ Go round a sharp left-hand bend, then at a footpath signpost, go right down a grassy path and cross a stone footbridge. Continue uphill to reach a bend on a track, just up from large granite houses.

> **WHERE TO EAT AND DRINK** ℹ
> There is a seasonal café at **Porthgwarra**, ideally located at the midway point in the walk. Porthcurno has several outlets including the **Beach Café** and the **Cable Inn**. A seasonal ice cream and soft drinks van is usually located in the Porthcurno car park.

⑤ Turn left, go over a stile beside a gate, then continue down a surfaced lane to **Porthgwarra Cove**. Opposite the shop and café, go right down a track, signposted '**Coast Path**' then follow the path round left in front of a house. Go sharp right at a junction and climb steps.

⑥ Continue along the coast path, partly reversing the previous route past Point ④. Keep right at junctions, and eventually descend past **St Levan's Well** to just above

> **WHILE YOU'RE THERE** ℹ
> The **Museum of Submarine Telegraphy** at Porthcurno, located above the top end of the car park, rewards a visit. It records the long history of undersea cable telegraphy. In its time, Porthcurno was the world's largest international cable station. The museum is contained within underground tunnels that served as a secret communications base during the Second World War.

Porth Chapel Beach. (Dogs should be kept under control on the beach.) Follow the coast path steeply over **Pedn-mên-an-mere**, and continue to the car park of the **Minack Theatre** (see What to Look For).

⑦ For the surefooted, cross the car park and go down the track to the left of the **Minack** compound, then descend the steep and dramatic cliff steps, with great care. When the path levels off, continue to a junction. The right fork takes you to **Porthcurno Beach** and back to the car park. The continuation leads to the road opposite the **Beach Café**, where a right turn leads to the car park. A less challenging alternative to the cliff steps is to turn left out of the Minack car park. Follow the approach road to a T-junction with a public road. Turn right and walk down the road, watching out for traffic.

> **WHAT TO LOOK FOR** ℹ
> The **Minack Theatre** was the unusual creation of Rowena Cade, whose family bought the rocky headland above Porthcurno Beach in the 1920s. A general interest in theatre led to the staging of Shakespeare's The Tempest on a makeshift stage on the cliffs in 1932. Miss Cade, ably assisted by skilled local gardeners and builders then developed the Minack over many years into a full scale theatre, carved out of the cliffs, a Cornish version in miniature of the great classical theatres of Greece and Rome, but with a stupendous backdrop. Today atmospheric performances of a variety of plays and musicals are staged during the summer months. A Minack performance is an unbeatable experience. Wine and light clothes for balmy summer evenings; full scale waterproofs and hot chocolate otherwise.

Wildflower Haven at Mullion

The heathland of the Lizard Peninsula supports some of the most remarkable of Britain's wild flowers.

•DISTANCE•	7 miles (11.3km)
•MINIMUM TIME•	4hrs
•ASCENT / GRADIENT•	164ft (50m) ▲ ▲ ▲
•LEVEL OF DIFFICULTY•	🚶 🚶🚶 🚶🚶
•PATHS•	Good inland tracks and paths, can be muddy in places during wet weather. Coastal footpath, 21 stiles
•LANDSCAPE•	Flat heathland and high sea cliff
•SUGGESTED MAP•	aqua3 OS Explorer 103 The Lizard
•START / FINISH•	Grid reference: SW 669162
•DOG FRIENDLINESS•	Dogs on lead through grazed areas. Notices indicate
•PARKING•	Predannack Wollas Farm car park (National Trust)
•PUBLIC TOILETS•	Mullion Cove, 200yds (183m) up road from harbour

BACKGROUND TO THE WALK

The heathland of the Lizard Peninsula near Mullion lacks the rugged beauty of Cornwall's granite moors; its flatness seems a dull contrast to the dramatic sea cliffs that define its edges; the only punctuation marks are the huge satellite dishes of the nearby Goonhilly tracking station and the lazily revolving blades of modern wind turbines. Yet, beneath the skin, this seemingly featureless landscape is botanically unique and exciting, not least because the Lizard's calcareous soil is rich in magnesium and supports plants that are more often seen in chalk or limestone regions. The warming influence of the sea and the area's generally mild and frost-free climate encourages growth.

Famous Plant

The Lizard's most famous plant is the Cornish heath, rare in Britain generally, but abundant on the Lizard. In full bloom it contributes to a glorious mosaic of colour, its pink and white flowers matched by the brilliant yellow of Western gorse and the deeper pinks of cross-leaved heath and bell heather. From the very start of the walk you are at the heart of the heathland. More common plants include spring squill, thrift and foxglove. Deeper into the heath are a variety of orchids including the rare green winged orchid, with its purple-lipped flowers.

Soapy Cove

Near the turning point of the walk you pass close to the old wartime Predannack airfield from where modern gliders soar into the air. Soon, the route joins the coast at Gew Graze, a feature that is also known as 'Soapy Cove' because of the presence of steatite, or soapstone. This is a fairly rare type of rock which was once used in the 18th-century production of china and porcelain. The final part of the route, along the cliffs to Mullion Cove, brings more flower spotting opportunities. On the path out of Gew Graze look for the yellow bracts and purple florets of carline thistle; the straw-coloured bracts curl over the flowerheads to protect them in wet weather.

Another remarkable plant is thyme broomrape, a dark reddish-brown, almost dead-looking plant that obtains its chlorophyll as a parasite growing on thyme. Such plants are often difficult to spot, whereas the smooth grassy slopes of the cliff tops near Mullion are a riot of powder blue spring squill, white sea campion and the yellow heads of lesser celandine and kidney vetch.

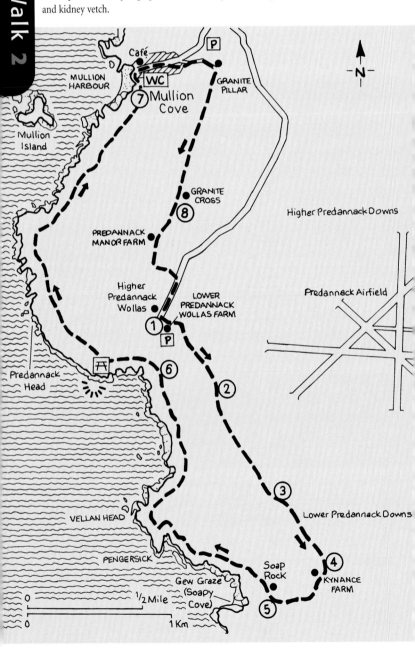

Walk 2 Directions

① Leave **Predannack Wollas Farm** car park by its bottom end. Follow the winding track ahead for just under ½ mile (800m) to where it ends at a gate. (Ignore a signposted track going off left just before this gate.) Beyond the gate, bear left to a stile. Follow the edge of the next field to a stile, then continue to open ground by a gate in a fence on the right.

② Go over the stile next to the gate, then bear away at an angle from the fence along a path to reach English Nature's **Kynance Farm Nature Reserve**. Keep ahead towards distant buildings.

③ Watch for a gap in the hedge on the left, go through the gap, then cross the next field to reach a rough track. Turn right along the track for a few paces then bear off left and follow the edge of the scrub.

④ Go through a gate, then follow a track going right. Merge with another track, and then in a few paces, and just before a ford, bear off to the right along a track towards the coast (**Kynance Farm** is up to the right).

⑤ At a crossing with the coast path, go right and steeply uphill, then go over a stile onto the cliff top. Follow the coast path as it winds round the edge of the often projecting cliffs at **Pengersick** and **Vellan Head**.

⑥ Go left at a junction, just past a National Trust sign for '**Predannack**'. (You can return to the car park by following the inland path from here.) Cross a stream in a dip and climb up left and continue along the coast path to **Mullion Cove** and Harbour.

⑦ Go up the road from **Mullion Harbour** and just beyond the public toilets and the shop, turn off right at a coast path sign. Keep to the right of the entrance to a holiday residential site and follow a track uphill. On a bend and just before a granite pillar, go off right and over a stone stile. Follow the path ahead through a grove of thorn trees and then through fields.

⑧ Pass a tall granite cross and then reach a lane and turn right along the lane towards the farm. Just before **Predannack Manor Farm** entrance, go left over a stile by a field gate, then turn right along the field edge. Go over a stile, then left along a hedged-in path, cross a stile and cross two fields to reach a lane (watch for traffic). Turn right to **Predannack Wollas Farm** car park.

WHERE TO EAT AND DRINK ⓘ

There is a café at Mullion Harbour, the **Porthmellin Café**, serving full cooked breakfast, morning coffee, cream teas, crab sandwiches, ice creams and soft drinks. Open Easter to September.

WHILE YOU'RE THERE ⓘ

Spend some time at **Mullion Harbour**. The harbour dates from the 1890s and is built like a little fortress for the good reason that the cove's position on the eastern shore of Mount's Bay leaves it open to the most ferocious storms from the west and south west. This western coast of the Lizard Peninsula was always known as a 'wrecking shore', especially in the days of sail when vessels rounding the opposite 'horn' of the bay, Land's End, could easily become 'embayed' if they did not set course properly to clear the Lizard. Once embayed in onshore storms, a sailing vessel was easily driven ashore. Mullion Harbour gave shelter to pilchard, crab and lobster fishing boats.

Walk 3

The Buzzards Walk

A wildlife walk along peaceful hillsides and riverbanks in mid Devon.

•DISTANCE•	3¾ miles (6km)
•MINIMUM TIME•	2hrs
•ASCENT / GRADIENT•	150ft (45m) ▲▲▲
•LEVEL OF DIFFICULTY•	🚶 🚶 🚶
•PATHS•	Waymarked paths, tracks and quiet lanes, 3 stiles
•LANDSCAPE•	Wooded hillsides and riverbanks
•SUGGESTED MAP•	aqua3 OS Explorer 114 Exeter & the Exe Valley
•START / FINISH•	Grid reference: SX 905121
•DOG FRIENDLINESS•	Dogs should be kept under control, livestock in some fields
•PARKING•	A narrow lane (No Through Road) leads to car park from B3137 near sign to Withleigh church
•PUBLIC TOILETS•	None on route

BACKGROUND TO THE WALK

There are three, little-known but nonetheless wonderful, areas of National Trust woodland – Cross's Wood, Thongsleigh Wood and Huntland Wood – tucked away in the secluded and undulating mid-Devon countryside to the west of Tiverton. This walk, in an area that is very much off the beaten track, explores these lovely woodlands draping over the steep hillsides above the valley of the tiny River Dart, which runs into the River Exe at nearby Bickleigh.

There are several excellent picnic spots along the route, the best one being reached at Point ④ where you can take a break on a high level open area after climbing up through Cross's Wood. It also gives you the opportunity to spend some quality time admiring that magnificent bird of prey so typical of this kind of landscape – the buzzard.

Buzzards

Watching a pair of common buzzards gliding effortlessly through the sky has to be one of the most magnificent sights above the hills and wooded valleys of the West Country. Using updraughts to soar overhead, their broad wings held forward and wing feathers extended, these most common of the larger raptors scan the ground below for their prey – small mammals, and rabbits in particular. Their characteristic 'whee-eur' call is frequently heard in hilly country, and if you're lucky enough to see one perched upright on a fence post you will notice it has a heavily barred tail, a small head and a black, hooked bill. Quite often you will see a lone buzzard being mobbed by crows. With the decline in persecution by gamekeepers, and with a plentiful supply of rabbits available, the buzzard population of the country now runs to tens of thousands.

By contrast the scarce honey buzzard is one of the country's rarest breeders. It lives on a diet of wild bees and their honey, as well as on other insects. This rather refined food source may be supplemented occasionally by small mammals. The honey buzzard is only a summer visitor to southern England, and fewer than a dozen pairs attempt to nest each year. They are very unusual in this part of Devon but have been spotted over the Haldon Hills to the south west of Exeter.

The woods, fields and banks encountered on this walk are full of interest all year round. As well as a glorious range of wild flowers, there is a fantastic babble of birdsong here in spring and summer, and a chance of seeing roe deer, and in the early evening perhaps a badger trundling along the path. You should also see dragonflies skimming over the sparkling waters of the Dart. The walk follows waymarked paths and tracks through the woodland, parts of which can be muddy at any time of year.

Walk 3 **Directions**

① From the car park cross the stile into a field, and turn right. At the hedge ahead turn left and walk towards the wood. Drop down steeply right, heading for the gate and a stone water trough near by.

② Once through the gate go straight ahead, keeping the hedge left. Cross the next stile and continue with the tiny **River Dart** on the right. Before the bridge turn left at the waymarker, through a small gate into another field. Turn right, keeping the high hedge right.

③ Leave the field through the next gate, which leads onto a broad track which rises through **Cross's Wood**. Soon after passing a bench a waymarker directs you left, off the

Walk 3

track and back into the woods up a fairly steep, narrow path, a little overgrown and muddy in places. Continue to climb until the path reaches a wide track at the top of the woods.

④ Turn right to follow the track gently downhill, through a gate into an open area where it zig-zags more steeply downhill between gorse, broom and bracken.

WHAT TO LOOK FOR
Deciduous woodlands such as these support a great variety of wild flowers. Shade-loving plants abound, but many early flowers bloom in spring before the leaf canopy shuts out too much light. Ancient woods are very stable plant communities, and some species such as ramsons – wild garlic – are evidence of old, undisturbed woodland. Look out too for primroses in early spring, and delicate wood anemones; then in May the carpet of bluebells so typical of this sort of habitat.

⑤ Continue on to the valley bottom and join the riverside track, passing through a gate with a sign asking horse-riders to dismount. Before the bridge ahead turn left on a broad track. After a few paces turn right over a stile and double-plank bridge to enter a field.

⑥ Keep the high hedge on your left and walk through the field for about 250yds (229m) to reach a small gate into **Huntland Wood**. Follow the path steeply uphill. It levels off and leads through the beautiful upper part of the wood before descending gradually to leave the wood at a lane.

⑦ Turn right and proceed downhill, cross the Dart at **Worthy Bridge**, turn right at the next junction and past some houses.

WHERE TO EAT AND DRINK
There is nothing very close by, but there are two pubs at Pennymoor, 5 miles (8km) further west. The **Cruwys Arms** is not open at lunchtime Monday to Thursday. The **Mount Pleasant** is open all day and serves good food. There's also the **Cadeleigh Arms** at Cadeleigh to the south of the walk, with real ale, excellent food and a pretty garden, but it's a bit of a trek along narrow, winding lanes to get there.

Where the lane bends left, go straight ahead through a gate onto a track, which you follow (with the river to your right) through a gate and into **Thongsleigh Wood**.

⑧ Continue along the track, with the river right. At a small gate leave the wood and enter some meadows; the path here is faint but continues straight ahead. The next gate (rather decrepit) leads onto a lane. Turn right over **Groubear Bridge** and climb back up the ancient rocky lane to the car park.

WHILE YOU'RE THERE
Take a trip to **Knightshayes Court**, signposted off the A396 at Bolham, 2 miles (3.2km) north of Tiverton. The family home of the Heathcoat Amorys, this splendid house looks down on Tiverton and on the site of the lace-making factory set up by industrialist John Heathcoat in 1815, which once employed 1,500 people, and from which the family gained their wealth. The house was begun in 1869 under John Heathcoat's grandson, and designed by William Burges. You really do get an impression of grand 19th-century country house life here. The gardens, which merge into woodland, are superb, especially in spring. There are some fine topiary animals on the box hedges near the house. The National Trust has established an excellent restaurant, shop and plant centre in the old stables.

The Birdlife of the Otter Estuary Nature Reserve

Discover a wealth of wildlife along the banks of the peaceful River Otter and the red sandstone cliffs towards High Peak.

Walk 4

•DISTANCE•	4¼ miles (6.8km)
•MINIMUM TIME•	2hrs
•ASCENT / GRADIENT•	164ft (50m) ▲ ▲ ▲
•LEVEL OF DIFFICULTY•	🚶 🚶 🚶
•PATHS•	Good level paths, coastal section and lanes, 2 stiles
•LANDSCAPE•	River meadow, cliffs and undulating farmland
•SUGGESTED MAP•	aqua3 OS Explorer 115 Exeter & Sidmouth
•START / FINISH•	Grid reference: SX 077830
•DOG FRIENDLINESS•	Opportunities for dogs to run free; some livestock
•PARKING•	By side of broad, quiet lane near entrance to South Farm
•PUBLIC TOILETS•	None on main route. Try Otterton Mill

BACKGROUND TO THE WALK

Peaceful, tranquil, lush, idyllic – these are all words that could easily be applied to this stroll along the banks of the River Otter. The river wends its way to meet the sea just east of Budleigh Salterton, its lower reaches a haven for a wealth of birdlife. In contrast to this, the walk continues along the top of the red sandstone cliffs typical of this area – but the coast path here is not in any way heart-thumpingly strenuous. The combination of the serene river meadows and the glorious coastal scenery – and then, perhaps, tea at Otterton Mill – make this an ideal family walk.

The Otter Estuary Nature Reserve

The Nature Reserve, south of White Bridge and managed by the Devon Wildlife Trust, is one of the smallest in the South West. The estuary was much more extensive in the past, and 500 years ago cargo ships could travel upriver as far as Otterton. Today the estuary provides a haven for all kinds of birdlife, best seen between October and March. Oystercatchers, dunlins and other wading birds come to feed here; large flocks of waders and ducks, such as wigeons and teal, attract peregrine falcons, sparrowhawks and mink. There are over 200,000 wigeon on British estuaries, and it is one of our most common over-wintering species of duck. Three-quarters of the estuary has been colonised by saltmarsh, which is also home to warblers in the summer months, linnets and greenfinches all year round, and kingfishers in winter. To catch the action, about ¼ mile (400m) from the start of the main walk take a small path right towards the river to a birdwatching hide, run by the Devon Birdwatching and Preservation Society. Stop for a while and watch the activity on the waters below – there's always something happening.

The mid-section of the walk brings us within sight of Otterton, a large, pleasant village, with many traditional cob and thatch buildings. The church – St Michael and All Angels – is most impressive. There was a Saxon church here before the Norman Conquest, rebuilt by Benedictine monks when they established a priory in the 12th century. The main monastery building lay on the north side of the church, and part of it – probably the guests' hall – remains today. After Henry VIII's Dissolution of the Monasteries, in 1539, the church gradually fell into disrepair until it was, eventually, totally rebuilt in the 1870s. The design was by Benjamin Ferrey and the funding came from the Rt Hon Louisa Lady Rolle, a local dignitary. The church today is extremely grand and spacious, with superb blue marble columns along the nave. The west tower is built of the Old Red Sandstone we saw in the cliffs earlier in the walk.

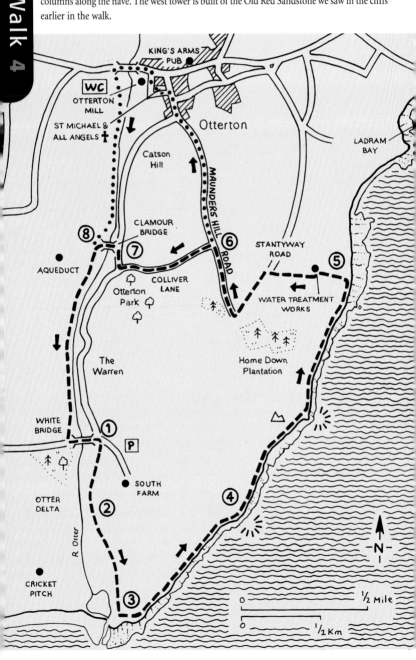

Walk 4

Walk 4 Directions

① Walk through the kissing gate to the right of the gate to **South Farm**. Turn right following signs for '**Coast Path Ladram Bay**'. The narrow, sandy path runs along the field edge, with lovely views right over the saltmarshes of the **Otter Estuary Nature Reserve** and the **River Otter**.

② At the end of that field a shallow flight of wooden steps leads to a walkway and footbridge, and up into the next field. There are good views downriver to the shingle bank at **Budleigh Salterton** and across the river to the cricket pitch.

WHILE YOU'RE THERE ⓘ

Visit **Bicton Park** and **Botanical Gardens**, straight over the B3178 from the road to Otterton. Bicton is open 364 days of the year, and has over 60 acres (24ha) of landscaped gardens, with a superb arboretum, lake and a secret garden, and a splendid 19th-century Palm House.

---

③ The path continues gently downhill until it turns sharply left following the line of the coast. Just before you turn east there are panoramic views right over the Otter delta, and along the beach.

④ After just over a mile (1.6km) the path rises a little, and you can see the whole of **Lyme Bay** ahead, including **High Peak** (564ft/157m – one of the highest points on the South Devon coast). Follow the coast path: the red sandstone cliffs are extremely friable and 'chunks' continually tumble seawards, but the path is safe. Pass through a small gate by the ruined lookout building, and downhill.

⑤ Turn left to leave the coast path on the '**Permissive path to Otterton**'; this narrow, grassy path leads over a stile; turn immediately left and follow the path right around the water treatment works, and up the gravelly lane to meet **Stantyway Road**. The lane veers right, but you should turn left up a grassy track, following signs to **Otterton** and the **River Otter**. The track soon veers right and gives way to a tarmac lane.

⑥ After 400yds (366m) **Colliver Lane** and the **River Otter** are signed to the left. Turn left here and follow a narrow, wooded green lane, which ends at a gate. Go through that, then almost immediately another, and follow the signs along the edge of the next field, which you leave over a stile onto a track.

⑦ Turn immediately left between two big ornamental brick pillars, and then right under a very large oak tree. Descend a short flight of steps and cross over the River **Otter** on **Clamour Bridge**, a wooden footbridge.

⑧ Turn left and follow the river south; over a small leat (look out for the aqueduct coming across the meadows on your right), through a gate and continue to **White Bridge**, where you go through a kissing gate, turn left and find your car.

WHERE TO EAT AND DRINK ⓘ

If you just do the main walk, drive up to the village of Otterton afterwards. The café at **Otterton Mill** is open daily from 10AM to 5PM (early closing in winter) and serves a great range of delicious wholefood dishes. The **King's Arms** (complete with its own post office) welcomes families, and has a beer garden and children's play area.

Horner's Corners

On the trail of Exmoor's red deer in the woodlands under Dunkery Beacon.

•DISTANCE•	4½ miles (7.2km)
•MINIMUM TIME•	2hrs 30min
•ASCENT / GRADIENT•	1,000ft (300m) ▲▲▲
•LEVEL OF DIFFICULTY•	🏃 🏃 🏃
•PATHS•	Broad paths, with some stonier ones, steep in places, no stiles
•LANDSCAPE•	Dense woodland in steep-sided stream valleys
•SUGGESTED MAP•	aqua3 OS Outdoor Leisure 9 Exmoor
•START / FINISH•	Grid reference: SS 898455
•DOG FRIENDLINESS•	Off lead, but be aware of deer and horse-riders
•PARKING•	National Trust car park (free) at Horner
•PUBLIC TOILETS•	At car park

BACKGROUND TO THE WALK

Horner takes its name from the Saxon 'hwrnwr', a wonderfully expressive word meaning snorer, that here describes the rumble of the stream in its enclosed valley. Above the treetops, Webber's Post is a splendid viewpoint out across the Bristol Channel. What Mr Webber stood there to view, though, was the hunting of red deer.

The herd on Exmoor numbers several thousand. Although this is small compared to those in the Scottish Highlands, the Exmoor stag himself is the UK's biggest wild deer. This is simply because his life is slightly easier – farmed deer are larger again. On Exmoor, as in the rest of Northern Europe outside Scotland, the deer remains a forest animal. Exmoor's mix of impenetrable woodland with areas of open grazing, even with all its houses, farms and fields, remains good deer country.

The calf is born dappled for camouflage under the trees, and lies in shelter during the day while the hind feeds. If you do come across a deer calf, leave it alone – it hasn't been abandoned. During the summer the stags and hinds run in separate herds. In the Scottish Highlands deer graze on high ground during the day to escape from midges, and descend to the forest at night; on Exmoor the main annoying pest is the human, so the deer graze the moor at dawn and dusk, and spend the day in the trees.

Stag Nights
In September and October comes the spectacular rut, when stags roar defiance at each other, and, if that fails, do battle with antlers for mating privileges. During this time they eat only occasionally, fight a lot and mate as often as possible. The stag with a mighty roar and a hard head can gather a harem of a dozen hinds. Your best chance of seeing one is very early or very late in the day – or else in the forest. I have had a bramble patch beside my path suddenly start bouncing around like an angry saucepan of milk, until, after ten seconds, a half-grown calf burst out of the middle of it and ran away. You may well smell the deer, even though it probably smelled you first and has already gone quietly away. Look closely, too, at the small brown cows two fields away – they may well be deer. I've seen grazing deer from a train window just five minutes out of Taunton Station, though they were the smaller roe.

While deer are thriving, it's the Exmoor stag hunters that are in danger of extinction. Just one pack of the traditional staghounds remains. Following pressure from its own members, the National Trust has banned hunting from its land, and the national government is set to ban it altogether when it finds the parliamentary time.

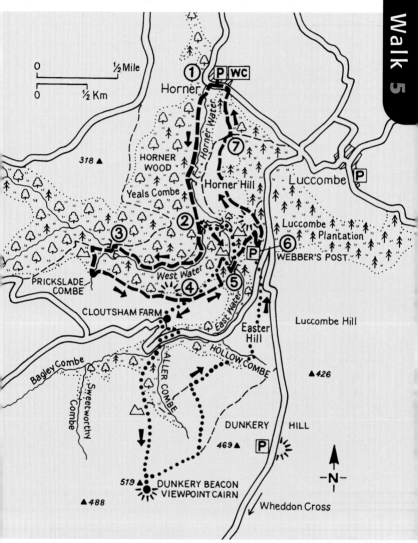

Walk 5 Directions

① Leave the National Trust car park in Horner village past the toilets and turn right to the track leading into **Horner Wood**. This crosses a bridge and passes a field before rejoining **Horner Water**. You can take a footpath alongside the stream instead of the track, they lead to the same place. Ignore the first footbridge, and continue along the obvious track to where a sign, 'Dunkery Beacon', points off to the left towards a second footbridge.

② Ignore this footbridge as well. Keep on the track for another 100yds (91m), then fork left on a path alongside **West Water**. This rejoins the track, and after another ½ mile (800m) a bridleway sign points back to the right. Here look down to the left for a footbridge. For me this was a thrilling balancing act on two girders – but the rebuilding of the bridge (swept away in floods) has now been completed.

③ Cross on to a path that slants up to the right. After 200yds (183m) turn left into a smaller path that turns uphill alongside **Prickslade Combe**. The path reaches the combe's little stream at a cross-path, with the wood top visible above. Here turn left, across the stream, on a path contouring through the top of the wood. It emerges into the open and arrives at a tree with a bench and a fine view over the top of the woodlands to **Porlock Bay**.

④ Continue ahead on a grassy track, with the car park of **Webber's Post** clearly visible ahead. Alas, the deep valley of the **East Water** lies

---

> **WHERE TO EAT AND DRINK** ⓘ
> Delightful Horner village has not one but two excellent **tea shops**, each with an outdoor seating area and ice creams. Those who would prefer beer or, of course, a glass of cider should head for the fleshpots of Porlock.

between you and your destination. So, turn down left on a clear path back into birchwoods. This zig-zags down to meet a larger track in the valley bottom.

⑤ Turn downstream, crossing a footbridge over the **East Water**, beside a ford. After about 60yds (55m) bear right on to an ascending path. At the top of the steep section turn right on a small sunken path that climbs gently to **Webber's Post** car park.

⑥ Walk to the left, round the car park, to a path marked 'Permitted Bridleway' to **Horner**. (Do not take the pink-surfaced, easy-access path immediately to the right.) After 80yds (73m) bear left on to a wider footpath. Keep ahead down a wide, gentle spur, with the deep valley of the **Horner Water** on your left. As the spur steepens, the footpath meets a crossing track signposted '**Windsor Path**'.

⑦ Turn right for perhaps 30 paces, then take a descending path signposted '**Horner**'. Narrow at first, this widens and finally meets a wide, horse-mangled track with wooden steps; turn left down this into **Horner**.

> **WHILE YOU'RE THERE** ⓘ
> **Dunster Castle** has everything – battlements and gardens, a wooded hill setting with an ancient village below, a working water mill, the national collection of strawberry trees (*Arbutus unedo*) and even a somewhat implausible King Arthur legend – he helped St Carantoc tame the local dragon.

> **WHAT TO LOOK FOR** ⓘ
> Multiple tree trunks growing from a single point show where the woodland has formerly been **coppiced**. Every ten years the new shoots would be cut back to the original stump. This method of harvesting a woodland is more productive than clear-felling and replanting, whether what you're after is oak bark for the tanning industry or just firewood. Coppicing has also allowed the original woodland plants to survive through the centuries.

Westhay Peatland Reserve

A nature ramble through reconstructed peat marshland, including a brief walk on water.

•DISTANCE•	4¾ miles (7.7km)
•MINIMUM TIME•	2hrs 15min
•ASCENT / GRADIENT•	250ft (80m) ▲ ▲ ▲
•LEVEL OF DIFFICULTY•	🚶 🚶 🚶
•PATHS•	Mostly smooth, level paths and tracks, 2 stiles
•LANDSCAPE•	Reed beds and water-meadows
•SUGGESTED MAP•	aqua3 OS Explorer 141 Cheddar Gorge
•START / FINISH•	Grid reference: ST 456437
•DOG FRIENDLINESS•	On leads in reserve, can be free on drove tracks
•PARKING•	Free car park at Decoy Pool, signposted from public road
•PUBLIC TOILETS•	None on route
•NOTE•	To bypass rough part, follow lane between Points ④ and ⑥

BACKGROUND TO THE WALK

At Westhay Moor the Somerset Trust for Nature Conservation (STNC) is carefully recreating the original peat wetland from a time before drainage and peat cuttings. This involves raising the water table with polythene barriers, and importing sphagnum moss and peatland plants from Cumbria. 'True blanket bog', one of their notices reminds us, 'should wobble when walked on...' And while these rehabilitated peat diggings are very good news for waterfowl and the nightjar, for rare spiders and the bog bush cricket, they are still a long way from the original Somerset moor.

Moor or Morass?

'Moor' is the same as 'mire' or 'morass'; the Saxon word first occurs in the account of King Alfred taking refuge at Muchelney. For the Saxons the moor was a place of mystery and fear. About 1,500 years ago the monster Grendel was the original 'Thing from the Swamp' in the poem of *Beowulf*. Open water alternated with reed beds and mud. The inhabitants moved around by boat, or by wading, or on stilts. Even if you could see out over the reeds it rarely helped as the mist would come down. And, at nightfall, the will o' the wisp misled you into the unstable mud, just in case you hadn't been swallowed up in it already.

If you did ever get out on to firm land, you were quite likely to be infected with ague or marsh fever. Even the modern name, 'malaria', reflects its supposed origin in the misty airs of the wetlands. Actually it was transmitted by mosquitoes that bred in the stagnant water. Oliver Cromwell, a fenman from East Anglia, died of malaria. It persisted in the marshes of Essex into the 20th century and may return with global warming in the 21st.

Wet Refuge

For those who knew its ways, the moor was the safest of refuges. Iron Age tribes built a village on wooden piles near Glastonbury; the Romans complained of the way the tribesmen would hide with only their heads above the water. Alfred found safety from the Danes here, as did the monks of Glastonbury.

Wealth in the Wet

The moor was also, in its own way, wealthy. The less wet sections grew a rich summer pasture, fertilised by the silt of the winter floods. It's no coincidence that Britain's most famous cheese comes from the edge of the Levels. The deep, moist soil also grew heavy crops of hemp. Henry VIII made the growing of this useful plant compulsory, as it supplied cordage and sailcloth for the navy. Today, under its Latin name of *Cannabis sativa*, it is, of course, strictly forbidden. The wetter ground yielded osiers for baskets and reed for thatch; wildfowl and fish; and goosefeather quills for penmen. Fuel was peat, or willow poles from the pollarded trees whose roots supported the ditches. And the rent for this desirable property was often paid in live eels.

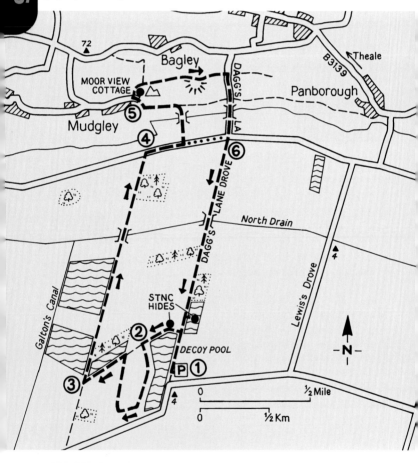

Walk 6 Directions

① Head into the reserve on a broad track, with **Decoy Pool** hiding behind reeds on the left. At the end of the lake a kissing gate leads to the STNC hide, with a broad path continuing between high reedbeds. Ignore a gate on the left ('No Visitor Access') but go through a kissing gate 60yds (55m) further on.

② A fenced track runs through peat ground, where birches are being felled to recreate blanket bog.

Walk 6

The track turns right; now take a kissing gate on the left for a path through trees. At its end a new track leads back through the peat. At the end turn left to reach a gate on to the next of the 'droves' or raised trackways through the peatland.

③ Turn right, passing hides and crossing a bridge over the wide **North Drain**; the land on each side now comprises water-meadows. The track leads to a lane.

④ If you wish to omit the field paths above (which are rough, but give a splendid view over the reserve), simply turn right, going along the road for 650yds (594m) to a junction, Point ⑥. Otherwise turn right as far as a right-hand bend, and continue for 175yds (160m) to where gates are on both sides of the road. Go through the left-hand one (with a red-painted marker) and cross to a gate and bridge over a ditch. Follow the left edge of the next field to its corner. Turn left through a gate and follow field edges to a small orchard. Turn right, up to the end of a tarred lane.

⑤ Turn left along the road to an uphill path to the left of **Moor View Cottage** – this becomes overgrown and quite steep – to a stile on the right. Cross the tops of five fields. In the sixth field drop slightly to pass below farm buildings (there is a helpful signpost here). A gate leads into a small orchard, with a

signposted gate on to **Dagg's Lane** just above. Turn down the lane to the road below.

⑥ Directly opposite Dagg's Lane is the track, **Dagg's Lane Drove**. This runs between meadows then re-enters the reserve, passing between pools left by peat extraction. Look out for a path on the left signposted to a hide. This leads out excitingly on stilts above the flooded mire. Return from the hide and rejoin the drove track, which quickly leads back to the car park.

Walk 7

Melbury Hill and Fontmell Down

A wildlife walk over the preserved downs around Compton Abbas, in search of butterflies and wild flowers.

•DISTANCE•	4½ miles (7.2km)
•MINIMUM TIME•	2hrs
•ASCENT / GRADIENT•	820ft (250m) ▲▲▲
•LEVEL OF DIFFICULTY•	☆☆ ☆☆ ☆☆
•PATHS•	Downland tracks, muddy bridleway, village lanes, 3 stiles
•LANDSCAPE•	Rolling downland with superb views
•SUGGESTED MAP•	aqua3 OS Explorer 118 Shaftesbury & Cranborne Chase
•START / FINISH•	Grid reference: ST 886187
•DOG FRIENDLINESS•	Some road walking
•PARKING•	Car park on road south of Shaftesbury, near Compton Abbas Airfield
•PUBLIC TOILETS•	None on route

BACKGROUND TO THE WALK

Since the end of the Second World War over 80 per cent of the chalk downs in England have been altered or lost because enriching artificial fertilisers have been introduced and land has been claimed for arable crops. Grazing is the key, in a scheme first introduced by the neolithic farmers. Without grazing, the close-cropped grass of the downs would soon revert to scrub and woodland. Modern management is therefore based on restoring the old farming cycles of grazing by sheep and cattle and maintaining the land for the benefit of threatened wildlife as well as for agricultural output. Preservation of the precious habitat of the outstanding area of Melbury and Fontmell Downs is in the hands of the National Trust with assistance from the Dorset Wildlife Trust.

Beautiful Butterflies

A chief beneficiary of this policy is the butterfly, for more than 35 species have been recorded here. Some have very specific requirements for their survival. The silver spotted skipper, for example, breeds in only 14 places in Britain, and only one in Dorset – Fontmell Down. They lay their eggs on the underside of sheep's fescue grass, but the grass has to be just the right length. If the juicy new grass shoots are nibbled by the sheep in August, the caterpillars will starve. Adonis blues are hardly less demanding – they need a tightly packed, south-facing, warm grassy slope. The grand-sounding Duke of Burgundy fritillary, on the other hand, likes to live on the edge – the edge of the sward, that is, where the cowslips blossom in springtime. (This need for a bit of rough may be a betrayal of its origin as the more humble 'Mr Vernon's small fritillary', for it was renamed in the 18th century.)

Wild Flowers

The wealth and variety of wild flowers found on these chalky downs is, of course, the other delight. They bloom unmolested, thriving on the poorer soils, not squeezed out by faster-growing monocultures. In summer look for the vivid violet-blue specks of early gentians in the turf, the tiny stalked spikes of the mauve milkwort and the deeper purple of thyme. They give way in autumn to the browny yellow flowers of the carline thistle and the spiralling, white-flowered spikes of autumn lady's tresses.

In autumn, this is a place to find glow-worms. About the length of a fingernail, these little creatures were once a common sight. It is the females who glow. Wingless and defenceless, they hide during the day, but at night crawl on to vegetation to shine their lower abdomens upwards to attract males flying by. The intense green pinpoint of light is caused by oxyluciferin, manufactured by specially adapted body cells which combine oxygen, water and an enzyme to emit light without generating heat.

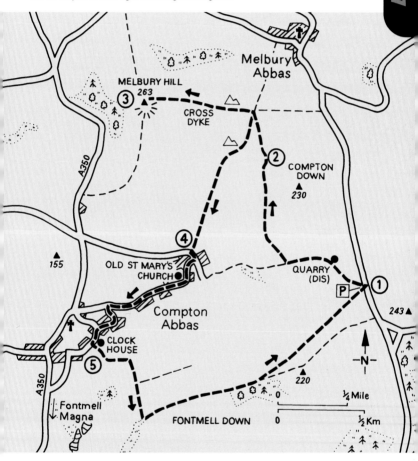

Walk 7 Directions

① Take the rough track from the bottom right corner of the car park, walking downhill towards **Compton Abbas**. Pass an old chalk quarry and continue downhill.

Soon turn right up some wooden steps and cross a stile to access **Compton Down**. Bear left and uphill towards a fence. Follow a track that contours round, just below the top of the hill, heading towards the saddle between the down and **Melbury Hill**.

Walk 7

② Pass a steep, natural amphitheatre on your left, go across the saddle and turn left at the fence. Follow this to the top of **Melbury Hill** – a steep climb but well worth it for the views. Pass the scar of an ancient cross dyke, on the left as you climb, and look down the other side to the silvery tower of Melbury Abbas church.

WHILE YOU'RE THERE ⓘ

Just east of here, over the border in Wiltshire, **Win Green Hill** (another National Trust property) is crowned by a ring of trees. It's the highest point of the ancient royal forest of Cranborne Chase, and the views are superb. When he tired of the hunt, King John hung out at nearby Tollard Royal.

③ A trig point marks the top of the hill, with fantastic views all around, including Shaftesbury on its ridge to the north and the ridges of Hambledon Hill to the south east. Retrace your route downhill, with views over Melbury Down and to Compton Abbas Airfield. Turn right on to the farm track. After a short distance bear left, down a steep path, to a gate. Go through this and bear immediately left through a

WHAT TO LOOK FOR ⓘ

As you walk towards Compton Abbas, pause at the churchyard of old **St Mary's**. Rest a moment on the great mounting block by the wall, to admire the ancient farmhouse opposite. All that remains of the old church is the ghostly, pale tower, blocked up and left to the pigeons. In the graveyard itself are some crumbling tombs and the weathered stump of an old cross. A new St Mary's was built within the village in 1866.

WHERE TO EAT AND DRINK ⓘ

Compton Abbas boasts the 17th-century **Milestones Tearoom**, just south of the church and accessible from the main road. It promises morning coffee, lunches and afternoon teas, and if the weather is sunny you can take it in the patio garden.

second gate. Go straight along the muddy field edge towards Compton Abbas. Pass through a gate and emerge on to a road.

④ Turn left and follow this road right round a sharp bend. Pass the tower of the original church, isolated in its small graveyard. Continue along the lane, passing houses of varying ages, with the spire of the modern church ahead in the trees. Descend between high hedges and turn left at the junction. Continue on this winding road through the bottom of the village, passing attractive, stone-built, thatched cottages.

⑤ Pass **Clock House** and turn left up the bridleway, signposted 'Gore Clump'. The gravel track gives way to a tree-lined lane between the fields. Go through a gate and continue straight on. Cross a stile by a gate and continue ahead along the edge of a field. In the corner, turn left along a fence and walk up the track above some trees to reach a gate. Pass through this on to **Fontmell Down**. Continue straight ahead on the rising track. After ½ mile (800m) ignore the stile to the right and keep straight ahead along the fence, to reach the top of the hill and a stile into the car park.

Studland's Sand and Heath

Easy walking through a significant nature reserve over beach and heath.

•DISTANCE•	7 miles (11.3km)
•MINIMUM TIME•	4hrs
•ASCENT / GRADIENT•	132ft (40m) ▲▲ ▲▲
•LEVEL OF DIFFICULTY•	🚶 🚶 🚶
•PATHS•	Sandy beach, muddy heathland tracks, verges, no stiles
•LANDSCAPE•	Sandy Studland Bay, heath and views over Poole Harbour
•SUGGESTED MAP•	aqua3 OS Explorer OL 15 Purbeck & South Dorset
•START / FINISH•	Grid reference: SZ 033835
•DOG FRIENDLINESS•	Not allowed on beach June–September, check locally for precise dates
•PARKING•	Knoll car park, by visitor centre, just off B3351
•PUBLIC TOILETS•	By visitor centre and near ferry toll station

BACKGROUND TO THE WALK

The glorious sands in Studland Bay are justly famous, attracting over one million visitors a year, so you'll need to get up early to have the beach to yourself. You're unlikely to be alone for long and local horseriders are often the first to arrive.

Naked Gape

As you progress up the beach, getting warmer, you can shed your clothes with impunity, for the upper stretch is the less familiar form of nature reserve, opening its arms to naturists. Even on a winter's morning you'll spot brave souls sunbathing naked in the shelter of the marram-covered dunes. Off-shore you'll see big, sleek motor boats – of the 'gin palace' variety – letting rip as they emerge from the constraints of Poole Harbour. Watch out, too, for the orange and blue of the Poole lifeboat on practice manoeuvres, and the yellow and black pilot boat nipping out to lead in the tankers. Jet skiers zip around the more sedate sailing yachts, all dodging the small fishing boats. It's a perfect seaside harmony, complete with 'wheedling' gulls.

Studland's sand is pale gold and fine-ground, trodden by thousands of feet, piled into hundreds of satisfying sand castles and smoothed daily by the sea. The shells underfoot become more numerous as you approach the tip of the sand bar. It's a wonderful opportunity for some shell spotting. Look for the flattish conical mother-of-pearl whorls of topshells, the curious pinky-brown pockets of slipper limpets, the glossy, uneven orange disks of the common saddle oyster and the flat reddish-brown sun-rays of scallops. The deeply ridged fans of common cockles and the vivid blue flash of mussels are a common sight. More challenging is to identify the uneven ellipse of sand gapers or the delicate finger-nail pink of the thin tellin.

Behind the beach lies the rugged heath, part of the same nature reserve, which is in the care of Natural England and the National Trust. These two bodies are currently working together on a programme of restoration. They are reclaiming heath that had become farmland, clearing scrub and maintaining controlled grazing to prevent it all reverting to woodland. I saw my first rare Dartford warbler here, perched on a sprig of gorse – with its pinky brown colouring and long tail, it's a distinctive little bird. All six of Britain's reptiles – common lizard, sand lizard, smooth snake, adder, grass snake and slow-worm – live on the heath. They may be spotted if you know where to look and what you're looking for. Be patient and you might see one soaking up the sunshine in a quiet corner. Trapped between the dunes and the heath is a freshwater lake known as the Little Sea. Hides allow you to watch the dizzying variety of coastal and freshwater birds which congregate here.

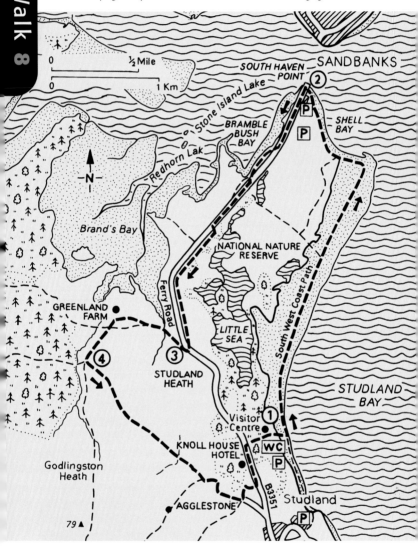

Walk 8 Directions

① From the car park go past the **visitor centre** to the sea. Turn left and walk up the beach for about

2 miles (3.2km). Marram-covered dunes hide the edge of the heath on your left, but you have views to Tennyson Down on the Isle of Wight, and the golden cliffs of Bournemouth curve away ahead.

Walk 8

Continue round the tip of the sand bar into **Shell Bay**. Poole opens out ahead – more precisely, the spit of Sandbanks, with the gleaming white Haven Hotel facing you across the harbour mouth. There are good views of the tree-covered nature reserve island of Brownsea, with Branksea Castle staring boldly out at the eastern end.

② Turn inland when you reach **South Haven Point**, joining the road by the phone box. Pass the boatyard and toll booth then bear right at a gate on to a bridleway, leading down to some houseboats. Turn left along the tranquil inner shore of **Poole Harbour** and past **Bramble Bush Bay**. Choose any of the various tracks that lead back up to the road. Cross over and follow the verge until the end of some woods on your left, when you can pick up the broad muddy track on the heath. After ½ mile (800m) this bends left, with views across to the Little Sea. Where the track bends sharply right to meet the road, stay straight ahead on the footpath for a few more paces.

③ Cross the road by a bus stop and head down the track, indicated by a fingerpost. Go past the marshy end of **Studland Heath** and up to a junction by **Greenland Farm**. Bear left and, just round the next corner, turn left through a gate on to the heath. Go straight along an old hedge-line, pass a barn on the left, and reach a fingerpost.

④ Turn left across the heath (not shown on the fingerpost), aiming for the distant lump of the **Agglestone**. Go through a gate by another fingerpost and continue along the muddy track over the top, passing the Agglestone away to your right. Go down into some woods, turn right over a footbridge and pass through a gate into a lane. Pass several houses then, where blue markers indicate a public bridleway, turn left into a field. Head diagonally right into a green lane and go through a gate at the bottom. Turn left along the verge, pass the Knoll House Hotel and turn right at the signpost to return to the car park.

Meon Valley Meander

Rising dramatically above the Meon Valley, Old Winchester Hill is a favoured haunt of historians and naturalists, and the start of this exhilarating walk.

•DISTANCE•	5½ miles (8.8km)
•MINIMUM TIME•	2hrs 15min
•ASCENT / GRADIENT•	472ft (144m) ▲▲▲
•LEVEL OF DIFFICULTY•	🚶 🚶 🚶
•PATHS•	Field paths, footpaths, tracks and sections of road, 9 stiles
•LANDSCAPE•	Chalk downland, gently rolling farmland and river valley
•SUGGESTED MAP•	aqua3 OS Explorer 119 Meon Valley
•START / FINISH•	Grid reference: SU 645214
•DOG FRIENDLINESS•	Let them off lead on Old Winchester Hill
•PARKING•	Natural England car park off Old Winchester Hill Lane
•PUBLIC TOILETS•	None on route

BACKGROUND TO THE WALK

Old Winchester Hill dominates the Meon Valley. From its summit, some 646ft (197m) above sea level, you can savour far-reaching views across the county, south across the Solent to the Isle of Wight, west to the New Forest and Wiltshire, and north to Beacon Hill. It's long been a natural vantage point, attracting early settlers who preferred the safety afforded by the high ground. The impressive remains of the fort you see today on the summit date back to the Iron Age. Its defences comprise a massive single bank and ditch enclosing about 14 acres (4 ha) with entrances at the east and west ends. The oval-shaped fort overlies a pattern of prehistoric fields and you will notice some large grassy mounds as you walk round the rampart. These are Bronze Age burial mounds, erected on the crest of the hill between 4,500 and 3,500 years ago for important members of society.

Nature Reserve

Old Winchester Hill was purchased by the state in 1954 and is now a National Nature Reserve, cared for by Natural England. The sheep-grazed chalk downland, with its mix of open grassland, scrub and woodland, is home to a number of rare butterflies and chalk-loving flowers. Walk this way in early summer and you will see the hill fort dotted with fragrant orchids, while in July look out for the bright blue round-headed rampion, a rarity in Britain, but which thrives here. On a warm August day the grassland is a sea of colour with hundreds of plants, flowers and wild herbs. In fact, an area just 1m (3ft) square can contain 30–40 different species of plant and over 200 species have been recorded on the reserve. The air shimmers with many thousands of chalkhill blue butterflies, feeding on the wild majoram, the plants on the reserve providing food for some 34 species of butterfly and their caterpillars. The longer grass is favoured by hedge and meadow browns and the beautiful marbled white butterflies. Bird-lovers should bring their binoculars, you may be lucky enough to see a peregrine falcon hunting, buzzards soaring high on the thermals, and summer migrants like the redstart and pied flycatcher. In winter, fieldfares and redwings feed in numbers on the abundant berries on the stunted juniper bushes, while the yew woods provide shelter to titmice and goldcrests.

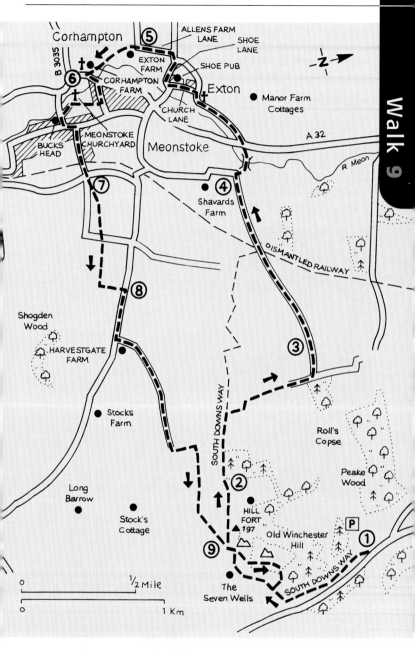

Walk 9 Directions

① From the car park go through the gate onto the open downland and turn left between the nature reserve's information boards.

Follow the path around the perimeter of the reserve. Merge with the **South Downs Way** (SDW) and bear right towards the hill fort. Pass through a gate, follow SDW markers left, then right across the centre of the hill fort.

② Descend and keep left at a fork by the rampart, heading downhill to a stile. Pass beneath yew trees and beside a gate. Continue downhill, then walk along the edge of a field and bear left onto a track. At a junction turn left along a track.

③ Where this enters a field, keep ahead along the stony path. Pass under the disused railway (in winter use the steps to cross the old track bed), and continue to a T-junction.

WHAT TO LOOK FOR ⓘ
Take a close look at **Corhampton Church**. Built on an artificial mound, it is remarkable in having no dedication, and has remained almost unaltered since it was built in the early 11th century. Many Saxon details can be seen, including characteristic 'long and short' stonework at the corners. Note too the sundial on the south wall (divided into eight sections not twelve), the 12th-century wall paintings in the chancel, the yew tree, said to be 1,000 years old, and the Romano-British coffin in the churchyard.

---

④ Bear right and cross the footbridge over the **River Meon** to the A32. Cross straight over into **Church Lane** and continue into Exton. Turn left along **Shoe Lane**, then right at the junction beyond the **Shoe** pub, and shortly bear left along **Allens Farm Lane**.

⑤ At a sharp right-hand bend, keep ahead along the path beside **Exton Farm**. Go through a gate and bear left along the right-hand edge of paddocks to a stile. Pass beside **Corhampton Farm** and **Church**, bearing left to the A32.

⑥ Cross over, walk left along the pavement and turn right by the shop. Take the metalled path beside the last house on your right and enter **Meonstoke churchyard**. Turn

---

WHERE TO EAT AND DRINK ⓘ
Good traditional pub food and Wadworth ales are served at the **Shoe** in Exton. The **Bucks Head** (open all day weekends) offers an extensive menu and B&B accommodation. Both pubs have delightful riverside gardens.

---

left along the lane to a T-junction beside the **Bucks Head**. Turn left, then left again at the junction. Follow the lane right (**Pound Lane**) and soon cross the old railway.

⑦ At a crossroads climb the stile on your left. Proceed ahead across the field and pass behind gardens, eventually reaching a stile and a lane. Climb the stile opposite and keep to the right-hand field edge to a stile. Maintain direction to a stile, then bear diagonally left towards a house and road.

⑧ Turn right and take the track left beside **Harvestgate Farm**. At the top of the track, bear left uphill along the field edge, then sharp right, following the path along the hedge into the next field. Cross the stile on your left into the **Nature Reserve** and ascend steeply to the hill fort ramparts.

⑨ Cross a stile and go right to join the outward route by the fort entrance. Through the gate opposite the information board, follow a path just beneath the downland rim. Bear right to a gate and retrace your steps to the car park.

WHILE YOU'RE THERE ⓘ
Visit **St John's churchyard** in nearby West Meon. Here you'll find the graves of Thomas Lord, the founder of Lord's cricket ground, who retired to the village in 1830, and that of Guy Burgess, the former British diplomat and Russian agent who died in Moscow in 1963.

Downlands to Brighstone

From the downland above Brighstone to the wild and beautiful shore.

•DISTANCE•	8¼ miles (13.3km)
•MINIMUM TIME•	4hrs
•ASCENT / GRADIENT•	941ft (287m) ▲ ▲ ▲
•LEVEL OF DIFFICULTY•	🏃 🏃 🏃
•PATHS•	Field and clifftop paths, woodland tracks, 10 stiles
•LANDSCAPE•	Farmland, chalk downland, woodland and coastal scenery
•SUGGESTED MAP•	aqua3 OS Outdoor Leisure 29 Isle of Wight
•START / FINISH•	Grid reference: SZ 385835
•DOG FRIENDLINESS•	Off lead on Mottistone Down, otherwise keep under control
•PARKING•	National Trust car park at Brookgreen
•PUBLIC TOILETS•	Brighstone

BACKGROUND TO THE WALK

The heart of old Brighstone is undoubtedly one of the prettiest village scenes on the island, full of old-world charm with thatched golden-stone cottages, tea gardens and a fine Norman church. It lies tucked away under the downland ridge in the centre of the south west coastal shelf, less than a mile (1.6km) from the coast, and the beautiful surrounding countryside is perfect for walking.

Microcosm of the Island

In fact, the varied nature of the landscape around the village is a microcosm of the island as a whole. Stroll south through the fields and you are on the wild and beautiful shore, with miles of sand and rock ledges. Puff your way north on to Brighstone Down, and you reach the largest area of forest on the island, dotted with Bronze Age and Neolithic burial mounds.

A sense of history pervades Brighstone, no more so following a visit to the tiny village museum. Here you will discover its notorious past. From the 13th century to the late 1800s, Brighstone was a noted smuggling village, with many of the local inhabitants involved in wrecking and contraband. Good money could be earned salvaging cargoes and timbers from ships wrecked along the nearby coast, and it was common for local children to seek credit from the Brighstone shopkeeper by promising 'Mother will pay next shipwreck'. It was not until the 1860s that a change of heart saw the first lifeboats being launched from Brighstone and Brook. Revd McCall aroused residents' consciences to Christian compassion for shipwrecked mariners, local benefactor Charles Seeley provided the finance, and reformed smuggler James Buckett, having served five years compulsory service in the navy as punishment for his crimes, became the first coxwain of the Brighstone boat.

The museum, or the Three Bishops pub come to that, will inform you that Brighstone is famous for the fact that three of its rectors were later appointed bishops. Thomas Ken was rector in 1667 and wrote the famous hymn 'Glory to thee, my God this night' before becoming Bishop of Bath and Wells. Samuel Wilberforce, son of the great anti-slavery campaigner William Wilberforce, was rector here for ten years (1830–40), founding the library and school, before being appointed Bishop of Winchester. Finally, in 1866, George Moberly arrived in the village, leaving three years later to become Bishop of Salisbury.

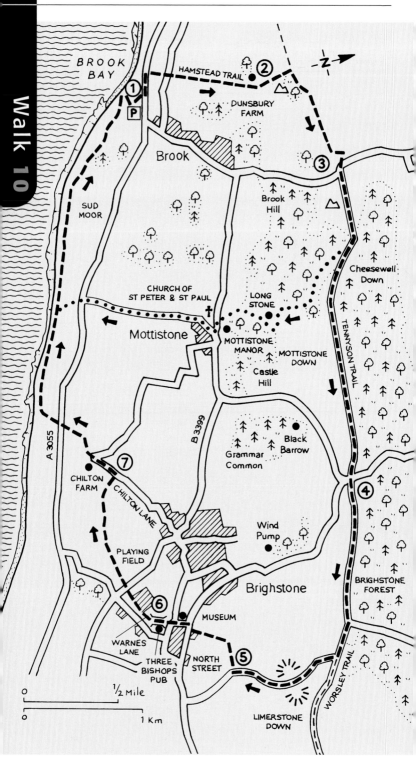

BROOK BAY

HAMSTEAD TRAIL

DUNSBURY FARM

Brook

SUD MOOR

Brook Hill

Cheesewell Down

CHURCH OF ST PETER & ST PAUL

LONG STONE

Mottistone

MOTTISTONE MANOR

MOTTISTONE DOWN

Castle Hill

Tennyson Trail

A 3055

B 3399

Black Barrow

Grammar Common

CHILTON FARM

CHILTON LANE

Wind Pump

Brighstone

BRIGHSTONE FOREST

PLAYING FIELD

MUSEUM

WARNES LANE

THREE BISHOPS PUB

NORTH STREET

Worsley Trail

LIMERSTONE DOWN

0

½ Mile

0

1 Km

Walk 10 Directions

① From the car park, turn left along the A3055 to a stile on the right, waymarked **Hamstead Trail**, and walk across the field to a track. Keep ahead beside cottages and maintain direction on reaching a crossing of tracks, heading uphill on a metalled track. Bear left then right around **Dunsbury Farm** to a T-junction.

② Turn right, then immediately left through a gate and ascend steeply between trees to a gate. Merge with a track at a junction and bear right. Go through a gate and continue to climb, shortly bearing right (marked by a blue byway sign) to follow the track downhill beside a line of telegraph poles. Keep right at a chalk track, go through a gate and cross the B3399 to a gate and bridleway, signed to **Shorwell**.

WHAT TO LOOK FOR
Mottistone Down is rich in wildlife, so look out for chalk-loving plants like rock roses, horseshoe vetch and the clustered bell flower that flourish here. There are some 30 species of butterfly that feed on the flowers, including chalkhill blues and dark-green fritillaries. In the forest you may see the native red squirrel.

③ Climb steadily across downland to a gate. Continue along the main track (**Tennyson Trail**) to the top of **Mottistone Down**. Descend to the car park and turn right along the lane. In a few paces turn left along a stony track.

④ Follow the **Worsley Trail** uphill beside **Brighstone Forest**. At the second junction of paths (by a fingerpost), take the bridleway right through a gate and descend

Limerstone Down on a gorse-edged path with superb views. On reaching a waymarker post, take the bridleway right for **Brighstone**.

⑤ Head downhill through bracken and join a sandy path between trees to **Brighstone**. Cross the lane, walk along **North Street**, passing the village museum, to the B3399. Turn left, then right beside the **Three Bishops** pub into **Warnes Lane**.

WHERE TO EAT AND DRINK
There's a **café** in Brook. The **Three Bishops** and a **tea room** in Brighstone, and a **coffee shop** in the Isle of Wight Pearl complex on the Walk 43. Afternoon teas are available from the **Summer House** at Mottistone Manor Garden.

⑥ Keep left of the car park along a metalled path to a road. Turn right, then left with a waymarker and cross a footbridge. Keep to the left-hand edge of the playing field and to the rear of gardens to a lane. Cross straight over and follow the fenced path to **Chilton Lane**.

⑦ Turn left, pass **Chilton Farm** and keep ahead at the sharp right-hand bend along a track to the A3055. Pass through the car park opposite and follow the path to the coast. Turn right along the coast path and soon cross a stile on to National Trust land ('**Sud moor**'). Keep to the coast path, crossing six stiles to reach **Brookgreen**. Bear right along beside the **Chine** and cottages and turn left to a stile and the car park.

WHILE YOU'RE THERE
Visit **Brighstone Village Museum**. Housed in an old thatched cottage, it features interesting mementoes of the village's history, particularly early school days and coastal themes like shipwrecks, smuggling and the village lifeboat.

Walk 10

Walk 11

The Snake River and the Seven Sisters

Follow a breezy trail beside the Cuckmere River as it winds in erratic fashion towards the sea.

•DISTANCE•	3 miles (4.8km)
•MINIMUM TIME•	1hr 30min
•ASCENT / GRADIENT•	Negligible ▲ ▲ ▲
•LEVEL OF DIFFICULTY•	🚶 🚶 🚶
•PATHS•	Grassy trails and well-used paths. Mostly beside the Cuckmere or canalised branch of river
•LANDSCAPE•	Exposed and isolated valley and river mouth
•SUGGESTED MAP•	aqua3 OS Explorer 123 South Downs Way – Newhaven to Eastbourne
•START / FINISH•	Grid reference: TV 518995
•DOG FRIENDLINESS•	Under close control within Seven Sisters Country Park. On lead during lambing season and near A259
•PARKING•	Fee-paying car park at Seven Sisters Country Park
•PUBLIC TOILETS•	Opposite car park, by visitor centre

BACKGROUND TO THE WALK

One of the few remaining undeveloped river mouths in the south-east, is the gap or cove known as Cuckmere Haven. It is one of the south coast's best-known and most popular beauty spots and was regularly used by smugglers in the 18th century to bring ashore their cargoes of brandy and lace. The scene has changed very little in the intervening years with the eternal surge of waves breaking on the isolated shore.

The Cuckmere River joins the English Channel at this point but not before it makes a series of extraordinarily wide loops through lush water-meadows. It's hardly surprising that this characteristic has earned it the occasional epithet 'Snake River'. Winding ever closer to the sea, the Cuckmere emerges beside the famous white chalk cliffs known as the Seven Sisters. Extending east towards Birling Gap, there are, in fact, eight of these towering chalk faces, with the highest one, Haven Brow (253ft/77m), closest to the river mouth. On the other side of the estuary rise the cliffs of Seaford Head, a nature reserve run by the local authority.

Seven Sisters Country Park

The focal point of the lower valley is the Seven Sisters Country Park, an amenity area of 692 acres (280ha) developed by East Sussex County Council. The site is a perfect location for a country park and has been imaginatively planned to blend with the coastal beauty of this fascinating area. There are artificial lakes and park trails, and an old Sussex barn near by has been converted to provide a visitor centre which includes many interesting exhibits and displays.

However, there is more to the park than these obvious attractions. Wildlife plays a key role within the park's boundaries, providing naturalists with many hours of pleasure and

Walk 11

enjoyment. The flowers and insects found here are at their best in early to mid summer, while spring and autumn are a good time to bring your binoculars with you for a close-up view of migrant birds.

A Haven for Birds

Early migrant wheatears are sometimes spotted in the vicinity of the river mouth from late February onwards and are followed later in the season by martins, swallows, whinchats and warblers. Keep a careful eye out for whitethroats, terns and waders too. The lakes and lagoons tend to attract waders such as curlews, sandpipers and little stints. Grey phalaropes have also been seen in the park, usually after severe autumn storms. These elusive birds spend most of their lives far out to sea, usually off South America or western Africa.

The walk explores this part of the Cuckmere Valley and begins by heading for the beach. As you make your way there, you might wonder why the river meanders the way it does. The meltwaters of the last Ice Age shaped this landscape and over the centuries rising sea levels and a freshwater peat swamp influenced the river's route to the Channel. Around the start of the 19th century, the sea rose to today's level and a new straight cut with raised banks, devised in 1846, shortened the Cuckmere's journey. This unnatural waterway controls the river and helps prevent flooding in the valley.

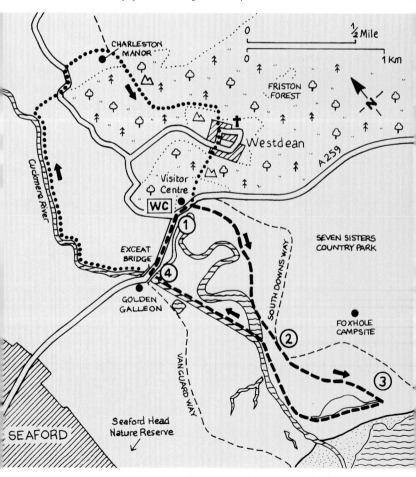

Walk 11

Walk 11 Directions

① Make for the gate near the entrance to the **Seven Sisters Country Park** and follow the wide, grassy path towards the beach. The path gradually curves to the right, running alongside a concrete track. The **Cuckmere River** meanders beside you, heading for the open sea. Continue ahead between the track and the river and make for a **South Downs Way** sign.

WHERE TO EAT AND DRINK ⓘ

The **Golden Galleon** by Exceat Bridge is a popular 18th-century inn thought to have inspired Rudyard Kipling's poem *Song of the Smugglers*. The menu is traditional English, with various Italian, Oriental and Indian dishes. The ales are supplied by the pub's own micro-brewery. The visitor centre at the **Seven Sisters Country Park** has a restaurant and tea rooms and in summer there is often an ice cream van in the car park.

---

② Avoid the long distance trail as it runs in from the left, pass it and the **Foxhole campsite** and keep ahead, through the gate towards the beach. Veer left at the beach and **South Downs Way** sign. On reaching the next gate, don't go through it. Instead, keep right and follow the beach sign. Pass a couple of wartime pill boxes on the left, an evocative reminder of less peaceful times, and go through a gate. Join a stony path and walk ahead to the beach, with the white wall of the **Seven Sisters** rearing up beside you.

WHAT TO LOOK FOR ⓘ

Shingle plants thrive on the sheltered parts of beaches and a stroll at Cuckmere Haven reveals the yellow horned-poppy and the fleshy leaved sea kale. Sea beet, curled dock and scentless chamomile also grow here.

---

③ Turn right and cross the shore, approaching a **Cuckmere Haven Emergency Point** sign. Branch off to the right to join another track here. Follow this for about 50yds (46m) until you come to a junction and keep left, following the **Habitat Trail** and **Park Trail**. Keep beside the Cuckmere and the landscape here is characterised by a network of meandering channels and waterways, all feeding into the river. Pass a turning for **Foxhole campsite** and follow the footpath as it veers left, in line with the **Cuckmere**. Make for a kissing gate and continue on the straight path by the side of the river.

④ Keep ahead to the road at **Exceat Bridge** and on the left is the **Golden Galleon** pub. Turn right and follow the A259 to return to the car park at the country park.

WHILE YOU'RE THERE ⓘ

If you have the time, take a look at the **Seaford Head Nature Reserve**, which lies on the west side of Cuckmere Haven. This chalk headland, which rises 282 ft (85m) above the sea, is a popular local attraction and from here the coastal views are magnificent.

Arlington's Lakeside Trail

Combine this delightful walk with a little birdwatching as you explore the banks of a reservoir by the Cuckmere River.

•DISTANCE•	3 miles (4.8km)
•MINIMUM TIME•	1hr 30min
•ASCENT / GRADIENT•	82ft (25m) ▲ ▲ ▲
•LEVEL OF DIFFICULTY•	🚶🚶 🚶🚶 🚶🚶
•PATHS•	Field paths and trail, some brief road walking, 13 stiles
•LANDSCAPE•	Level lakeside terrain and gentle farmland
•SUGGESTED MAP•	aqua3 OS Explorer 123 South Down Ways – Newhaven to Eastbourne
•START / FINISH•	Grid reference: TQ 528074
•DOG FRIENDLINESS•	Mostly on lead – as requested by signs en route
•PARKING•	Arlington Reservoir
•PUBLIC TOILETS•	At car park

BACKGROUND TO THE WALK

It was in 1971 that Arlington's rural landscape changed in both character and identity. A new reservoir was opened, supplying water to the nearby communities of Eastbourne, Hailsham, Polegate and Heathfield. Study the blurb on the grassy bank and you'll learn that the area of the reservoir is equivalent to 121 football pitches and that the maxium depth of the lake is 37ft (11.3m), deep enough to submerge four single decker buses.

Fishing

The 120-acre (46ha) reservoir was formed by cleverly cutting off a meander in the Cuckmere River and it's now an established site for wintering wildfowl, as well as home to a successful rainbow trout fishery. Besides the trout, bream, perch, roach and eels make up Arlington's underwater population. Fly fishing is a popular activity here and the lake draws anglers from all over Sussex.

The local nature reserve was originally planted with more than 30,000 native trees, including oak, birch, wild cherry, hazel and hawthorn. The grassland areas along the shoreline are intentionally left uncut to enable many kinds of moth and butterfly to thrive in their natural habitats. Orchids grow here too.

Bird Watching

Arlington Reservoir, a designated Site of Special Scientific Interest (SSSI), is a favourite haunt of many birds on spring and autumn migrations and up to 10,000 wildfowl spend their winter here, including large numbers of mallard and wigeon. The shoveler duck is also a frequent visitor and most common as a bird of passage. You can identify the head of the shoveler drake by its dark, bottle-green colouring and broad bill. The breast is white and the underparts bright chestnut, while its brown and black back has a noticeable blue sheen. The female duck is mottled brown.

Great crested grebes, Canada geese and nightingales are also known to inhabit the reservoir area, making Arlington a popular destination for ornithologists. See if you can spot the blue flash of a kingfisher on the water, its colouring so distinctive it would be hard to confuse it with any other bird. It's also known for its piercing whistles as it swoops low over the water. The reservoir and its environs are also home to fallow deer and foxes, so keep a sharp look-out as you walk around the lake.

The walk begins in the main car park by the reservoir, though initially views of the lake are obscured by undergrowth and a curtain of trees. Be patient. After visiting the village of Arlington, where there is a welcome pub, the return leg is directly beside the water, providing a constantly changing scenic backdrop to round off the walk.

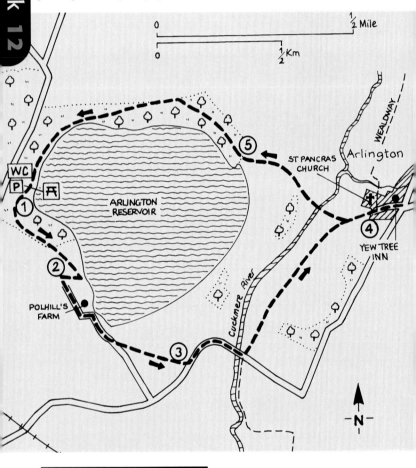

Walk 12 Directions

① From the car park walk towards the information boards and then turn right to join the waymarked bridleway. Cut through the trees to a tarmac lane and look for a bridleway sign. Follow the lane and soon the reservoir edges into view

again. On reaching a gate signed 'No entry – farm access only' bear right and follow the bridleway and footpath signs.

② Skirt the buildings of **Polhill's Farm** and return to the tarmac lane. Turn right and walk along to a kissing gate and a '**circular walk**' sign. Ignore the gate and keep on

---

WHERE TO EAT AND DRINK ℹ️

Arlington Reservoir has a **picnic site** by the car park where you can relax before or after the walk. The **Yew Tree Inn** at Arlington has a children's play area, beer garden and a choice of home-cooked dishes. Lunch and dinner are served every day and there is a choice of real ales. Nearby is the **Old Oak Inn,** originally the village almshouse and dating from 1733. The likes of Newhaven cod in batter, curry and steak-and-kidney pudding feature on the menu.

---

the lane. Continue for about 100yds (91m) and then branch left over a stile into a field. Swing half right and look for a second stile to the right of a pond. Cross a third stile and go across a pasture to a fourth.

③ Turn left and follow the road as it bends right. Cross the **Cuckmere River** and then bear left to join the **Wealdway**, following the sign for **Arlington**. Walk along the drive and when it curves to the right, by some houses, veer left over a stile. The spire of **Arlington church** can be seen now. Continue ahead when you reach the right-hand fence corner, following the waymark. Cross several stiles and a footbridge. Keep to the right of the church, cross another stile and pass the **Old School** on the right.

WHILE YOU'RE THERE ℹ️

Stop off at the **Arlington bird hide**, opened in 1996, and see if you can identify members of Arlington's feathered population. In spring you might spot an osprey, a large bird which occasionally visits lakes, fens and estuaries and preys almost exclusively on fish. Look out too for house martins, sand martins, sandpipers, blackcaps, kestrels, mallards and dunlins – among other birds. If you are interested in ornithology, a visit to the bird hide is a must.

---

④ Walk along the lane to the **Yew Tree Inn**, then retrace your steps to the church and cross the field to the footbridge. Turn right immediately beyond it to a stile in the field corner. Cross the pasture to the obvious footbridge and continue to a second footbridge where there are two stiles. Head across the field towards a line of trees, following the vague outline of a path. The reservoir's embankment is clearly defined on the left, as you begin a gentle ascent.

WHAT TO LOOK FOR ℹ️

Call into Arlington's **St Pancras Church**. One of the most interesting churches in Sussex, it's built of flint and the nave dates back to Saxon times. Look closely and you can see that there are many examples of different architectural styles. Buy a copy of the guide to the church to enable you to learn more about this fascinating place of worship.

---

⑤ Cross a stile by a galvanised gate and go through a kissing gate on the immediate right. Follow the path alongside the lake and pass a bird hide on the left. Turn left further on and keep to the bridleway as it reveals glimpses of the lake through the trees. Veer left at the fork and follow the path alongside the **reservoir**.

Butterflies Over Dover

An exhilarating wildlife trail over Dover's famous white cliffs.

•DISTANCE•	5½ miles (8.8km)
•MINIMUM TIME•	2hrs 30min
•ASCENT / GRADIENT•	131ft (40m) ▲▲▲
•LEVEL OF DIFFICULTY•	林 林 林
•PATHS•	Chalky cliff paths, some sections of road
•LANDSCAPE•	Grassy clifftops with extensive sea views
•SUGGESTED MAP•	aqua3 OS Explorer 138 Dover, Folkestone & Hythe
•START / FINISH•	Grid reference: TR 321412
•DOG FRIENDLINESS•	Good, but best to start from clifftop car park with a dog
•PARKING•	Russell Street and St James Lane, also on cliffs by National Trust tea room
•PUBLIC TOILETS•	Dover and National Trust tea room

BACKGROUND TO THE WALK

Go on, admit it. As soon as you saw that this walk took you over those famous white cliffs you came over all Vera Lynn and hummed, 'There'll be bluebirds over the white cliffs of Dover,' to yourself. It's okay, practically everyone who walks here does the same at some point. Yet while this distinctive landmark is known all over the world and is seen as a symbol of England, few people realise that it is also an important wildlife habitat – so important that it supports species that are rarely found elsewhere in the country.

The Chalk Downland

The cliffs, which are made of chalk, are topped with a thin, porous soil that has been grazed by animals for hundreds of years, creating what is known as chalk downland. Grazing stops coarse grasses and scrub invading the land and creates the ideal environment for hundreds of wild flowers to flourish. And while the early farmers didn't realise it, they were creating unique plant communities. While you're walking, keep your eyes peeled for plants like horseshoe vetch, early spider orchid and yellow rattle that gets its name from the seed pods that rattle in the wind. And with wild flowers, of course, come butterflies – particularly those wonderful blue ones that you so rarely see these days. Look out for the silvery chalkhill blue and the gorgeous sapphire Adonis blue. I even spotted a butterfly here in December. It wasn't close enough to identify, but it was a cheering sight nonetheless.

Grazing Ponies

Other wild creatures of the cliffs include adders (you're unlikely to see one, they hide from people), slow worms (not a snake but a legless lizard), common lizards and birds such as fulmars, peregrine falcons and skylarks – no bluebirds though.

Unfortunately modern farming methods have led to a 98 per cent decline in chalk downland and with it, of course, a similar decline in the plants and animals it supports. In an attempt to halt this decline, the National Trust has introduced Exmoor ponies to the white cliffs. These hardy little ponies eat the coarse grasses that would otherwise invade the land, and so allow the wild flowers to grow.

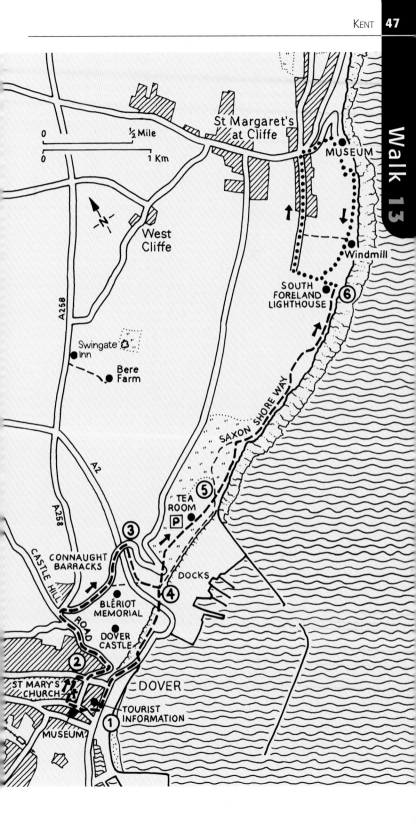

Walk 13

Walk 13 Directions

① From the **tourist information centre** on the front, walk to the right and at a roundabout go up **Bench Street**. At a crossing turn left into the market square. **Dover Museum** is just to the left. Turn up the road on the right. Keep going to **St Mary's Church** and then turn right along the path that runs beside the church. Keep ahead through the car park, cross some water and come out on to **Maison Dieu Road**.

WHILE YOU'RE THERE ⓘ

Dover Castle was built by the Normans after the Conquest in 1066 to control the native population. But the site, high above the sea, has an even more ancient history. There was an Iron-Age hill fort here and the Romans used the site to defend this part of their empire. Inside the castle you can see the remains of the Pharos, a beacon, which helped to guide the Roman fleet into the harbour.

---

② Turn right here, and then left, steeply, up **Castle Hill Road**. Eventually pass the entrance to **Dover Castle**. Further on, just past **Connaught Barracks**, turn right along Upper Road, signed 'Blériot Memorial'.

③ Cross the bridge over the main road and then take the footpath on the right. Go down some steps, fork left and, in a few paces, fork right.

Continue on this track and eventually emerge from the scrub to see the sea.

④ Turn left here, walk up some steps, with docks on your right. At a National Trust car park follow the **Saxon Shore Way** down to the right and over the cliffs. Continue past the coastguard station to a gate.

⑤ The path now continues along the cliffs and up to **South Foreland Lighthouse**. Some of the tracks branch off and lead very close to the cliffs – but there is a danger of cliff falls so keep to the main route. You may see some Exmoor ponies on this part of the walk. They've been introduced to the cliffs to graze the rare chalk downland and help preserve the habitat.

⑥ At **South Foreland Lighthouse** turn around and retrace your steps along the cliff – no hardship when you have these views. You can take the upper path here and walk past the **National Trust tea room** if you fancy stopping for tea. Otherwise continue down the steps and walk under the main road. Go along **Athol Terrace**, past the **First and Last** pub, and up on to the main road and back to the start point.

WHERE TO EAT AND DRINK ⓘ

The **National Trust tea room** on the cliffs is the best place to stop. You can get tea, scones and cakes or something more substantial, like a hot sandwich.

WHAT TO LOOK FOR ⓘ

Early on in this walk you'll pass a sign for the **Blériot Memorial** and, as it's only a short distance off the main route, it's worth a visit. The memorial commemorates the first successful flight across the English Channel. The *Daily Mail* set a challenge to early aviators offering £1,000 to the first person who could cross the Channel by plane. The prize was won by Frenchman Louis Blériot (1872–1936), who flew from France on 25 July 1909 in a single-engined plane and crash-landed not far from Dover Castle. The flight lasted 37 minutes.

With the Wetland Birds of Barnes

Discover the wildlife of the award-winning London Wetland Centre and join the course of the Oxford and Cambridge Boat Race.

•DISTANCE•	3¾ miles (6km)
•MINIMUM TIME•	1hr 30min
•ASCENT / GRADIENT•	Negligible ▲▲▲
•LEVEL OF DIFFICULTY•	🚶 🚶 🚶
•PATHS•	Riverside tow path, muddy after rain
•LANDSCAPE•	Views across Thames
•SUGGESTED MAP•	aqua3 OS Explorer 161 London South
•START / FINISH•	Grid reference: TQ 227767; Barnes Bridge rail ¾ mile (1.2km) or bus 283 (known as 'the Duck Bus') from Hammersmith tube
•DOG FRIENDLINESS•	London Wetland Centre (LWC) is no-go area for dogs
•PARKING•	At LWC (pay if not visiting)
•PUBLIC TOILETS•	At London Wetland Centre

BACKGROUND TO THE WALK

Rowing boats, like birds, glide gracefully through water and also, like birds, you'll see plenty of them during this easy walk. Barnes has long been associated with the Oxford and Cambridge Boat Race. Indeed, the footbridge, added in 1895, was specifically designed to hold the crowds watching the last stage of the 4⅓ mile (7km) race to Mortlake.

Loads of Birds

The riverside functions rather like a wildlife highway, providing a natural habitat for birds. There are plenty of them to see without having to put a foot inside the London Wetland Centre (LWC) – but to omit it would be to miss out on a very rewarding experience. So why not extend the walk and visit the LWC? There are more than 2 miles (3.2km) of paths and 650yds (594m) of boardwalk to explore once you have paid the admission charge.

Four Reservoirs and a Vision

The mother hen of all bird sanctuaries is the Wildfowl and Wetlands Trust at Slimbridge in Gloucestershire. It was founded by Sir Peter Scott, son of the great explorer, Scott of the Antarctic. One of his father's diaries carries the words: 'teach the boy nature' and this was indeed achieved, for Peter Scott became a renowned painter and naturalist. In recognition of his achievements, a larger-than-life sculpture of him stands on a raised gravel island at the entrance to the LWC, the only inner city wetland reserve in the world.

There are now nine wetland centres in the UK. This one began with four redundant reservoirs owned by Thames Water. They formed a partnership with the housing developer, Berkeley Homes and donated £11 million to help construct the centre. The 105 acre (43ha) project took five years to complete. In 2001 the centre won the British Airways *Tourism for Tomorrow* award.

Walk 14

Once inside, there are three main sections: world wetlands, reserve habitats and waterlife. The first contains captive birds from around the world – North America is accessed via a log cabin complete with authentic furniture. There are information panels too. One of them contradicts the popular belief that swans mate for life. Another tells us about meadowsweet, which is found in damp woods and marshes and used in herbal teas, mead flavouring and even air fresheners.

A Chorus of Facts

Back to birds, and why do they make so much noise? The dawn chorus is their way of telling other birds where they are – 'keep off my patch!' is the message – but it's also to attract a mate. Some birds with colourful plumage find this easy, but others have developed a distinctive song to attract attention, of which the cuckoo is a good example.

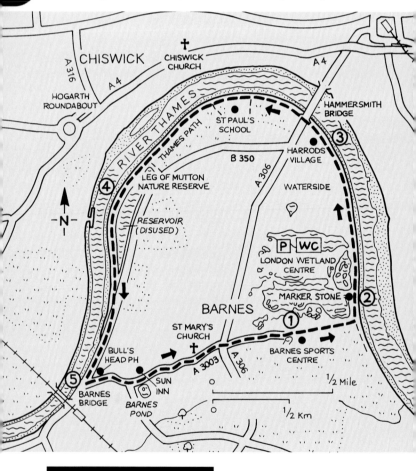

Walk 14 **Directions**

① Turn left out of the **London Wetland Centre** and follow the path, initially to the left of the

Barnes Sports Centre and then beside some sports fields. At a T-junction turn left along the well-signposted **Thames Path**, alongside the river in the direction of Hammersmith Bridge.

② About 100yds (91m) along the path on the left is a stone post, denoting the 1 mile (1.6km) marker of the Oxford and Cambridge University Boat Race. Steve Fairbairn, who was born in 1862, founded the Head of the River Race and this was the start of the world-famous, annual boat race that traditionally takes place in March.

WHILE YOU'RE THERE ⓘ

Chiswick church could once be reached by a ferry across the Thames, but since 1934 the only way is by bridge. The artist William Hogarth (from whom the Hogarth Roundabout takes its name) is buried in the churchyard. At the rear of the Sun Inn is **Barnes Bowling Club**, where Sir Francis Drake is said to have taught Elizabeth I the game of bowls.

---

③ The landscaped area of smart flats on the left is called **Waterside** and, a few paces further, a red brick building bears the name Harrods Village. Once past this, as if replicating the trademark Harrods colours of green and gold, is **Hammersmith Bridge**. Follow the path past **St Paul's School**, where *Planets* composer Gustav Holst was a music teacher. On the opposite side of the river, Chiswick Church's green roof is visible.

④ Turn left through a wooden gate into the **Leg of Mutton Nature Reserve**. Continue along the path to the right of this stretch of water, which was once a reservoir. When

---

WHAT TO LOOK FOR ⓘ

The development, **Waterside**, was constructed by Berkeley Homes after the company purchased 25 acres (10ha) and built the luxury homes that have a unique, bird's eye view of the centre and its wildlife. Adjacent, the **Harrods Village** building was once used to store furniture by those taking up posts in the British Empire. Derelict, it was also sold to Berkeley Homes and it now contains 250 flats with green window frames. Even the security guard wears a Harrods green and gold uniform.

---

the path swerves to the left, leave by a wooden gate to the right. Turn left and follow the riverside path towards **Barnes Bridge**.

⑤ Just past the **Bull's Head** pub turn left into **Barnes High Road**. At the next junction, by the little pond, bear left into **Church Road**. Past the **Sun Inn** is a row of village shops and 100yds (91m) further on, the lychgate to **St Mary's Church**. At the traffic lights continue ahead to return to the **London Wetland Centre** and the start of the walk.

WHERE TO EAT AND DRINK ⓘ

Unlike many on-site cafés, the **Water's Edge Café** at the London Wetland Centre is a delight. It's bright and spacious, serves good quality soups, sandwiches, salads and cakes, and has outdoor seating on large, wooden tables with umbrellas. There are also newspapers to read. The south-facing **Sun Inn** on Church Road, opposite Barnes duck pond lives up to its name – it's quite a suntrap in summer. The usual home-cooked food with a choice of vegetarian options is available here, as is a selection of Tetley's ales and Fuller's London Pride, which is brewed in nearby Chiswick.

Deer Old Richmond Park

A walking wildlife safari through Europe's largest city park, Richmond Park.

•DISTANCE•	6¾ miles (10.9km)
•MINIMUM TIME•	2hrs 30min
•ASCENT / GRADIENT•	164ft (50m) ▲ ▲ ▲
•LEVEL OF DIFFICULTY•	林林 林林 林
•PATHS•	Mainly tarmac paths
•LANDSCAPE•	Parkland and deer
•SUGGESTED MAP•	aqua3 OS Explorer 161 London South
•START / FINISH•	Grid reference: TQ189728; Richmond Station (tube and rail) 1½ miles (2.4km)
•DOG FRIENDLINESS•	Will love it but keep on lead near deer
•PARKING•	Car park at Pembroke Lodge in Richmond Park
•PUBLIC TOILETS•	Pembroke Lodge

BACKGROUND TO THE WALK

Richmond Park was once a royal hunting ground and, even today, it retains this upper crust image. Covering 2,500 acres (1,013 ha), it is a wonderful mix of panoramic views, wildlife havens and landscaped plantations, which are worth seeing in all seasons. For the most part, the walk follows the Tamsin Trail, a 7½ mile (12.1km) leisure path that runs around the perimeter of the park and that is for the sole use of walkers and cyclists.

The 750 or so deer are free to wander in the parkland, much of which has remained unchanged for centuries. Cars are allowed in certain areas of the park – it's not unusual for drivers to have to wait for a few minutes while a herd of deer crosses the road in front of them – but the best way to observe these beautiful creatures is on foot. There are two types of deer in the park – red and fallow deer. The males and females of red deer are stags and hinds, and of fallow deer are bucks and does. Red deer are indigenous to Britain, but fallow deer were introduced about 1,000 years ago. Norman hunters preferred the fallow for its grace and beauty.

Although there are enough plants to provide a nutritional diet for deer, acorns, horse chestnuts and sweet chestnuts also help to build up fat reserves during the winter months. During the rut (from September to November) the stags can often be seen fighting and herding the hinds into small breeding groups. Give them a wide berth if you pass them during the walk and keep your dog on a lead, to avoid alarming them. Culls, although the least favourite part of a gamekeeper's job, are necessary not only to prevent overgrazing but also to help maintain the park's reputation for having some of the best herds in the world.

If you see a bird that would look more at home in the sub-tropics than London, it's probably a ring-necked parakeet. These colourful birds, which have very long, pointed wings, were brought into Britain from Africa and India in the 1960s and sold as pets. Those that managed to escape began to breed successfully in the wild, and, despite the colder climate of Britain, their numbers are increasing. Noise from groups can sometimes be heard from the treetops in Richmond Park. They love to eat crab apples in summer and sycamore seeds during the rest of the year. Although they do not represent a problem to other birds, fruit growers may not be so fond of them.

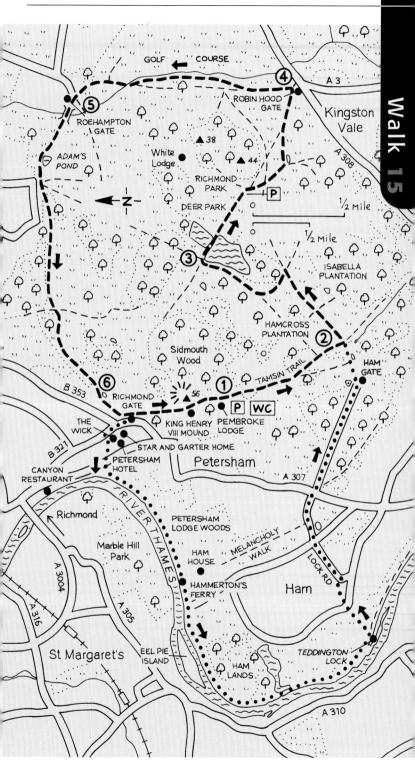

GOLF ← COURSE

④

ROBIN HOOD
GATE

Kingston
Vale

A 3

⑤
ROEHAMPTON
GATE

ADAM'S
POND

White
Lodge

▲ 38

▲ 44

RICHMOND
PARK

P

A 308

←Z—

DEER PARK

½ mile

½ mile

③

ISABELLA
PLANTATION

HAMCROSS
PLANTATION

②

Sidmouth
Wood

TAMSIN TRAIL

HAM
GATE

B 353

⑥
RICHMOND
GATE

▲ 56

①

P WC

PEMBROKE
LODGE

THE
WICK

KING HENRY
VIII MOUND

B 321

STAR AND GARTER HOME

Petersham

CANYON
RESTAURANT

PETERSHAM HOTEL

A 307

Richmond

R I V E R   T H A M E S

PETERSHAM
LODGE WOODS

Marble Hill
Park

HAM
HOUSE

MELANCHOLY
WALK

LOCK RD

Ham

A 3004

A 305

HAMMERTON'S
FERRY

St Margaret's

EEL PIE
ISLAND

HAM
LANDS

TEDDINGTON
LOCK

A 316

A 310

Walk 15

Walk 15 Directions

① From the car park at **Pembroke Lodge** turn right to follow the **Tamsin Trail** in the general direction of **Ham Gate**. The path veers to the right and later runs close to the road.

② At a crossroads leading to Ham Gate, turn left past the **Hamcross Plantation**. At the next crossroads turn right to visit the **Isabella Plantation**, otherwise continue and turn left at the next main junction, before another plantation, and circle the wood clockwise along a wide track. Turn right at the next junction and follow the path to the end of the pond.

WHILE YOU'RE THERE ⓘ

The Isabella Plantation was originally planted with oaks in 1831, but it now has three large ponds, a stream, a collection of rare trees and some magnificent azaleas. You'll be surprised how many people don't know that this is here – and you can't blame the ones that do for not sharing their secret, as this is a very special place, especially in the early morning.

③ Turn right along a path between the two ponds and continue ahead, ignoring paths branching off that would lead you to a car park. After this, turn right and follow the road that swings to the left towards

Robin Hood Gate. Deer are often spotted here but their coats give them good camouflage, especially against a background of bracken.

WHAT TO LOOK FOR ⓘ

In the formal garden of Pembroke Lodge is the highest point in the park, **Henry VIII Mound**. This prehistoric burial ground is not easy to find (take the higher path past the cottage) but well worth the effort, for here is a view of the dome of St Paul's Cathedral through a keyhole of holly. The cathedral may be 10 miles (16.1km) away from the avenue of sweet chestnuts in the park but this is better than any optical illusion, and the view is also conserved. The King was said to have stood on this mound while his second wife, Anne Boleyn, was being beheaded at the Tower of London.

④ Turn left at Robin Hood Gate. Follow the gravel path of the **Tamsin Trail** past the **Richmond Park Golf Course** and on to **Roehampton Gate**.

⑤ Continue over a footbridge and, after a further 500yds (457m), the path winds to the right of **Adam's Pond**, which is one of the watering holes used by the deer. Follow the path across the upper end of the park, past **Sheen Gate**, to **Richmond Gate**.

⑥ Turn left at **Richmond Gate** and continue along the path to reach **Pembroke Lodge** and the start of the walk.

WHERE TO EAT AND DRINK ⓘ

Pembroke Lodge, designed by Sir John Soane, was the childhood home of Bertrand Russell. Its views over west London towards Windsor are vast (although Windsor Castle is hard to spot). The tea room offers hot dishes and snacks and has seating outside on the terrace in fine weather. Just before Richmond Bridge is **Canyon**, where south west London meets Arizona. There is seating outside near a funky cactus terrace, complete with giant maple tree; entry is through two of the largest wooden doors this side of Phoenix. The menu includes chargrilled tuna, lamb cutlets and various salads. Sunday brunch is very popular.

Island Views from the Marloes Peninsula

An easy wildlife walk around a windswept headland overlooking two offshore islands and a marine nature reserve.

•DISTANCE•	6 miles (9.7km)
•MINIMUM TIME•	2hrs 30min
•ASCENT / GRADIENT•	420ft (128m) ▲ ▲ ▲
•LEVEL OF DIFFICULTY•	👫 👫 👫
•PATHS•	Coast path and clear footpaths, short section on tarmac, 10 stiles
•LANDSCAPE•	Rugged cliff tops and beautiful sandy beaches
•SUGGESTED MAP•	aqua3 OS Explorer OL36 South Pembrokeshire
•START / FINISH•	Grid reference: SM 761089
•DOG FRIENDLINESS•	Poop scoop on beaches
•PARKING•	National Trust car park above Martin's Haven, near Marloes village
•PUBLIC TOILETS•	Marloes village

BACKGROUND TO THE WALK

The Marloes Peninsula forms the westernmost tip of the southern shores of St Brides Bay. The paddle-shaped headland is a popular place to walk due to the narrow neck that affords minimum inland walking for maximum time spent on the coast. It is famous for its stunning scenery, which includes two of the Pembrokeshire Coast National Park's finest and least-crowded beaches, some secluded coves that are often inhabited by seals, and wonderfully rugged coastline. There are also fine views over a narrow but turbulent sound to the small islands of Skomer and Skokholm – two significant seabird breeding grounds. The walking is captivating, even by Pembrokeshire standards.

Wildlife Sanctuary

Skomer is the largest of the Pembrokeshire islands and is one of the most significant wildlife habitats in the whole country. The island, separated from the mainland by the rushing waters of Jack Sound, measures approximately 1½ miles (2.4km) from north to south and 2 miles (3.2km) from east to west. It was declared a National Nature Reserve in 1959 and, as well as the protection it receives as part of the National Park, it's also designated as a Site of Special Scientific Interest (SSSI), a Special Protection Area (SPA) and a Geological Conservation Review Site (GCR). Much of the land is a Scheduled Ancient Monument, courtesy of a number of clearly visible Iron-Age settlements and enclosures. If that's not enough of an accolade, the sea that surrounds the island is a Marine Nature Reserve, one of only two in the United Kingdom; the other is Lundy, off the North Devon coast.

Puffins and Shearwaters

The two stars of the Skomer show are the diminutive but colourful puffin and the dowdy and secretive Manx shearwater. Puffins need little introduction; their colourful beaks and

Walk 16

clown-like facial markings put them high on everybody's list of favourite birds. There are around 6,000 nesting pairs on Skomer. They arrive in April and lay a single egg in a burrow. The chick hatches at the end of May and the adult birds spend the next two months ferrying back catches of sand eels for their flightless offspring. After around seven weeks of this lavish attention the chick leaves the nest, usually at night, and makes its way to the sea. Assuming that it learns to look after itself successfully, it will spend the next few years at sea, only returning when it reaches breeding maturity.

Bashful Birds

The mouse-like shearwater is slightly larger than the puffin but it also lays its single egg in a burrow, overlooking the sea. It may not be as obviously endearing as its painted neighbour, especially as most visitors to the island never actually see one, but it's a beautiful and fascinating bird in its own right and there are in fact around 150,000 pairs on Skomer, Skokholm and Middleholm; which amounts to about 60 per cent of the world's total population. The reason they are seldom seen is because they are fairly vulnerable to predators on land so they leave the nest at dawn and spend the whole day at sea, not returning to their burrow until it's almost dark. A careful seawatch at last light may reveal them gathering in huge rafts just offshore or even endless lines of flying birds returning to the island – against the sunset, it's quite a magical sight.

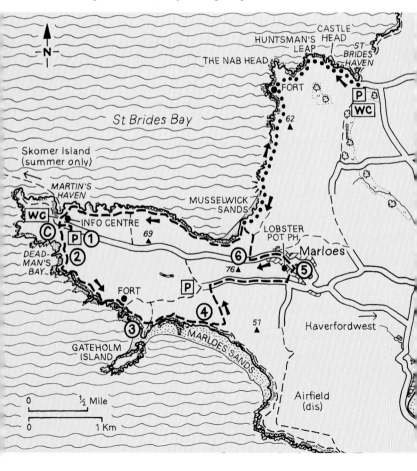

Walk 16 Directions

① From the car park turn left on to the road and walk down to the bottom of the hill. Bear around to the left, then go through the gate straight ahead into the **Deer Park**. Turn left and follow the path along to a stile and out on to the coast.

WHILE YOU'RE THERE ⓘ

If you have a day to spare then **Skomer Island** is well worth a visit. The *Dale Princess*, a 50-seat passenger boat, departs Martin's Haven regularly every morning during summer and returns during the afternoon. As well as the wildlife and the relics of ancient civilisations, there's also some fine walking. Note that dogs are not allowed on the island.

② With the sea to your right, continue easily along over **Deadman's Bay** to another stile. The next section cruises along easily, passing the earthworks of an Iron-Age fort on the left and crossing another stile as you approach **Gateholm Island**.

③ It is possible to get across to the island at low tide, but care is needed to scramble over the slippery rocks. To continue the walk, follow the coast path, above the western end of the beautiful **Marloes Sands** until you drop easily to the main beach access path.

④ Turn left and climb up to the road; turn right here. Follow the road along for around ¾ mile (1.2km) to a bridleway on the left. Follow this down and turn left into **Marloes** village.

⑤ Pass the **Lobster Pot** on the left and continue ahead to leave the village. Ignore a few tracks on the right, as the road bends around to the left, and continue out into open countryside where you'll meet a footpath on the right.

⑥ Walk down the edge of the field and bear around to the left to drop back down on to the coast path above **Musselwick Sands**. Turn left and follow the path west for over 1½ miles (2.4km) to **Martin's Haven**. Meet the road and climb past the information centre back to the car park.

WHERE TO EAT AND DRINK ⓘ

The **Lobster Pot** in Marloes is conveniently placed at the halfway point of the walk, but no dogs or muddy boots, please. Alternatively, head for **Dale** or **Little Haven** at the end of the walk as both offer better options.

WHAT TO LOOK FOR ⓘ

If you're walking along the coast in spring or summer you'll not fail to be impressed by the small white and pink flowers that carpet the cliff tops. These are **sea campion** (white) and **thrift** (pink), both common along the Pembrokeshire coast.

As you approach Musselwick Sands, you should be able to see a small island some 8 miles (12.9km) offshore. This is Grassholm and during the summer months it appears almost pure white. It isn't due to the colour of the rock but 30,000 breeding pairs of **gannets** that return to the island every year. Unlike the puffins and shearwaters of Skomer, the gannets are easily spotted, usually in small flocks, cruising a few hundred yards out looking for fish. If you spot them, watch closely and you'll probably witness their spectacular dive as they fold in their wings and plummet like darts into the water.

Walk 16

Pounding the Sound with a Hermit Monk

Along the shores of Ramsey Sound with great views and excellent wildlife-spotting opportunities.

•DISTANCE•	3½ miles (5.7km)
•MINIMUM TIME•	2hrs
•ASCENT / GRADIENT•	197ft (60m) ▲ ▲ ▲
•LEVEL OF DIFFICULTY•	🚶 🚶 🚶
•PATHS•	Coast path and easy farmland tracks, 5 stiles
•LANDSCAPE•	Undulating coast, dramatic views to Ramsey Island
•SUGGESTED MAP•	aqua3 OS Explorer OL35 North Pembrokeshire
•START / FINISH•	Grid reference: SM 724252
•DOG FRIENDLINESS•	One dog-proof stile and farmyard
•PARKING•	Car park above lifeboat station at St Justinian's
•PUBLIC TOILETS•	Nearest at Porth Clais or Whitesands

BACKGROUND TO THE WALK

This is one of the easiest walks, but it's also one of the most rewarding, with drop-dead gorgeous coastal scenery and plenty of chances to spot some of Pembrokeshire's varied wildlife. On a calm summer's day, the bobbing boats in Ramsey Sound display the kind of tranquillity you'd usually associate with a Greek island. See it on a rough day, with a spring tide running, and the frothing, seething currents that whip through the narrow channel are frightening to say the least. If the views aren't enough, a keen eye and a handy pair of binoculars may well produce sightings of seals, porpoises, dolphins, choughs and even peregrine falcons.

St Justinian

St Justinian was a hermit from Brittany who became the abbot of St David's Cathedral and acted as St David's confessor. Disillusioned with the lethargic attitude of the monks, he absconded to Ramsey Island to establish a more spiritual community. Some of his more loyal monks travelled with him, but eventually even they became fed up with his strict regimes and chopped off his head. It is said he walked back across Ramsey Sound carrying it in his arms.

His remains were buried in the small chapel on the hillside overlooking the sound, which bears his name. Later, St David took them to his own church. St Justinian is revered as a martyr, his assassins are thought to have been under demonic influence, and his life is celebrated on 5 December each year.

Ramsey Island

Less than 2 miles (3.2km) long and 446ft (136m) high at its tallest point, Ramsey Island is a lumbering humpback ridge separated from the St David's coast by a narrow sound. Known in Welsh as Ynys Ddewi – St David's Isle – this is the place where, legend suggests, St David met St Patrick.

It's a haven for wildlife and has belonged to the RSPB as a nature reserve since 1992. The eastern coast looks pretty tame, but the western seaboard boasts some of Pembrokeshire's tallest and most impressive cliffs, punctuated with sea caves and rock arches that are the breeding grounds of the area's largest seal colony. At its narrowest point, a string of jagged rocks protrude into the sound. These are known as The Bitches and they make a terrifying spectacle indeed. Tides gush through the rocks at speeds of up to 8 knots, creating a scene that resembles a mountain river in spate. The resultant waves and eddies make an extreme salt-water playground for white-water kayakers. Looking slightly out of place against the salty ocean backdrop, the island is populated by a herd of red deer.

Harbour Porpoises

Ramsey Sound is one the best places to catch a glimpse of Pembrokeshire's shyest marine mammals, harbour porpoises. Resembling dolphins, though never more than 7ft (2.1m) in length, small schools of these tiny cetaceans crop up all around the coast, but are frequently seen feeding in the currents at either end of the sound. Unlike dolphins, they seldom leap from the water, but their arched backs and small dorsal fins are easy to spot as they surface for air. Choose a day when the water is fairly flat, then scan the ocean from a promontory like Pen Dal-aderyn with a pair of binoculars. Once you spot one, you should find it easy to see others.

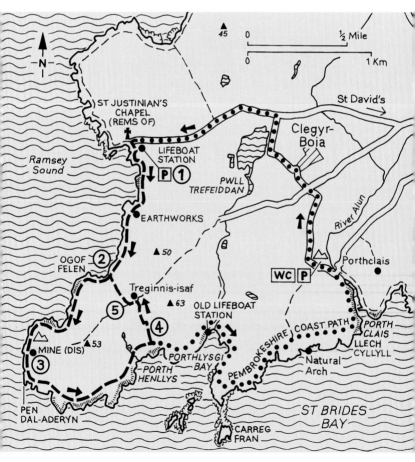

Walk 17 Directions

① Walk down to the lifeboat station and turn left on to the coast path, above the steps. Follow this, passing above a number of lofty, grassy promontories that make great picnic spots. After ½ mile (800m), look out for the traces of Iron-Age earthworks on the left.

WHAT TO LOOK FOR ⓘ
Take a second look at any of the small crows you see as you follow this stretch of coast path. What appears at first glance to be a jackdaw is probably sporting a sharp red bill and bright red legs and is one of Britain's rarest crows, the **chough**. These small birds are incredibly common in Pembrokeshire, however, where they nest on ledges and feed mainly on insects.

② Pass a gate and a track on your left – this is your return route – and swing around to the west above **Ogof Felen**. This is a good seal pup beach in autumn. The trail climbs slightly and then drops steeply to a ruined copper mine, directly opposite **The Bitches**.

③ Continue easily to **Pen Dal-aderyn** and then swing eastwards to enter **St Brides Bay**. The path climbs above some magnificent cliffs and passes between a few rocky outcrops before veering north above the broad bay of **Porth Henllys**. Drop down into a shallow valley until you come to a fingerpost at a junction of paths.

WHILE YOU'RE THERE ⓘ
Take a **boat trip** around Ramsey Island. As well as getting a close-up look at the seal colonies on the western flanks, you'll also get a great view of the rushing waters of The Bitches. Wear waterproofs as it can get pretty wet.

④ Turn left and cross a stile on the right, into a field. Turn left to follow the track along the wall to another gate, where you enter a courtyard. Keep left here and pass a barn on the left. When the track opens out into a field, keep right to pass through a gate and on to a waymarked track.

WHERE TO EAT AND DRINK ⓘ
There are plenty of options in St David's, but the **Low Pressure Café** in the High Street is probably the most popular, especially with surfers, climbers and walkers. It's inexpensive and does great sandwiches and cakes. For pub food and a drink, the **Farmers Arms** in Goat Street, has got to be a favourite.

⑤ Follow this waymarked track down between dry-stone walls to reach another gate, which leads back out on to the coast path. Turn right and retrace your outward route along the grassy clifftop path back to **St Justinian's**.

An Invigorating Trundle Around Strumble

A walk in some of the wildest countryside of the Pembrokeshire coast.

•DISTANCE•	8 miles (12.9km)
•MINIMUM TIME•	3hrs 30min
•ASCENT / GRADIENT•	920ft (280m) ▲▲▲
•LEVEL OF DIFFICULTY•	🚶🚶 🚶
•PATHS•	Coast path, grassy, sometimes muddy tracks, rocky paths, 21 stiles
•LANDSCAPE•	Rugged headland, secluded coves and rocky tor
•SUGGESTED MAP•	aqua3 OS Explorer OL35 North Pembrokeshire
•START / FINISH•	Grid reference: SM 894411
•DOG FRIENDLINESS•	Care needed near livestock
•PARKING•	Car park by Strumble Head Lighthouse
•PUBLIC TOILETS•	None on route

BACKGROUND TO THE WALK

This is my favourite stretch of the Pembrokeshire coast, although at times it feels like 'coast path meets the Himalayas', as the narrow ribbon of trail climbs and drops at regular intervals throughout. This is the real wild side of Pembrokeshire.

High Cliffs

The headland cliffs tower above the pounding Atlantic surf, the path cuts an airy, at times precarious, line across their tops and the sky is alive with the sound of seabirds. Atlantic grey seals, porpoises and even dolphins are regularly spotted in the turbulent waters. Garn Fawr, a formidable rocky tor that lords high above the whole peninsula, brings a touch of hill walking to the experience, and the shapely lighthouse flashes a constant reminder of just how treacherous these spectacular waters can be.

Beacon of Light

Built in 1908 to help protect the ferries that run between Fishguard and Ireland, the Strumble Head Lighthouse guards a hazardous stretch of coast that wrecked at least 60 ships in the 19th century alone. The revolving lights, which flash four times every 15 seconds, were originally controlled by a massive clockwork system that needed rewinding every 12 hours. This was replaced in 1965 by an electrically powered system and the lighthouse was then converted to unstaffed operation in 1980. It's possible to cross the daunting narrow chasm that separates Ynys Meicel (St Michael's Island), where the lighthouse stands, from the mainland by a rickety bridge.

Atlantic Grey Seals

This is one of the best walks in Pembrokeshire to spot these lumbering marine giants that reach over 8ft (2.4m) in length and can weigh as much as 770lbs (350kg). They are usually seen bobbing up and down (bottling) in the water just off the coast, but in autumn when the females give birth to a single pup, they often haul up on to inaccessible beaches where the young are suckled on milk with an incredibly high fat content. The pups shed their white coat after around three weeks, when they are then weaned and taught to swim before being abandoned. The males are usually bigger than the females, with a darker coat and a much more pronounced 'Roman' nose. The best places to see seals on this walk are the bays of Pwll Bach and Pwlluog, near the start.

Walk 18 **Directions**

① Walk back up the road and cross a stile on the left on to the coast path. Pass above the bays of **Pwll**

Bach and **Pwlluog**, then drop steeply to a footbridge behind the pebble beach of **Porthsychan**.

② Follow the coast path waymarkers around **Cnwc Degan**

Walk 18

and down to another bridge, where a couple of footpaths lead away from the coast. Continue along the coast, passing a cottage on the right and climbing and dropping a couple of times, before you reach the obelisk at **Carregwastad Point**.

③ Follow the track inland and cross a stile on to a track, where you turn right, away from the coast path. Continue with the path up through the gorse to a wall, then turn right on to a good track. Take this through a succession of gates and around a left-hand bend.

④ Ignore a track to the right and continue up the cattle track to the farmyard where you swing right and then left, after the buildings, to the road. Turn right and follow the road past a large house to a waymarked bridleway on the left.

Pass **Trenewydd** and go through a gate on to a green lane. Follow this up to another gate and on to open ground.

⑤ Turn right here and follow the wall to yet another gate. This leads to a walled track which you follow to the road. Turn left and climb up to the car park beneath **Garn Fawr**. Turn right, on to a hedged track, and follow this up, through a gap in the wall, and over rocks to the trig point.

⑥ Climb down and cross the saddle between this tor and the other, slightly lower, one to the south. From here head west towards an even lower outcrop and pass it on the left. This becomes a clear path that leads down to a stile. Cross this and turn left, then right on to a drive that leads to the road.

⑦ Walk straight across and on to the coast path. Bear right and cross a stile to drop down towards **Ynys y Ddinas**, the small island ahead. Navigation is easy as you follow the coast path north, over **Porth Maenmelyn** and up to a cairn.

⑧ Continue along the coast, towards the lighthouse, until you drop to a footbridge above **Carreg Onnen Bay**. Cross a stile into a field, then another back on to the coast path and return to the car park.

Take a Walk on the Wild Side

A tough walk, but one that really explores the more austere side of the Welsh uplands and the wildlife that lives there.

•DISTANCE•	9½ miles (15.3km)
•MINIMUM TIME•	6hrs
•ASCENT / GRADIENT•	2,000ft (610m) ▲ ▲ ▲
•LEVEL OF DIFFICULTY•	𝍫 𝍫 𝍫
•PATHS•	Riverside path, faint or non-existent paths over moorland, some good tracks, 4 stiles
•LANDSCAPE•	Stunning valley, remote moorland, some forestry
•SUGGESTED MAP•	aqua3 OS Explorer 200 Llandrindod Wells & Elan Valley
•START / FINISH•	Grid reference: SN 863533
•DOG FRIENDLINESS•	Care needed near livestock
•PARKING•	Lay-by on minor road by bridge over Afon Gwesyn or by WC ¼ mile (400m) to south west (grid ref SN 859861)
•PUBLIC TOILETS•	At car park near start
•NOTE•	Avoid in poor visibility

BACKGROUND TO THE WALK

This is the toughest walk in the whole book, but more by the nature of the terrain than the amount of ascent. The rewards, for those who are prepared to navigate their way carefully over one short stretch of trackless moorland, are rich beyond description, for this is a foray into the wilder side of Wales – a place that sees few footprints. For less experienced walkers, this is definitely one to tackle only after you've cut your teeth on the high ground of the Brecon Beacons, and then only in good visibility. Alternatively, if you're unsure about the navigation, or if you are in any doubt about the visibility, follow the outward leg on to Drygarn Fawr and return by retracing your steps.

The Red Kite
The remote nature of the landscape links this area, more than any other, with one of Britain's most beautiful birds, the red kite. It was the scene of this most majestic raptor's final stand. Free of persecution, pesticides and disturbance, a mere handful defiantly resisted extinction by scavenging these moors and nesting in the abundance of trees that line the valleys. Their decline was thankfully halted by a number of conservation groups who, working closely with local landowners, started a release programme of birds imported from Scandinavia and Spain. Successful breeding in both England and Scotland began in 1992 and since then the population has increased significantly.

The birds are easily distinguished from the more common buzzard, which can also be seen in this area, as they are much slimmer in build with narrower, more angular wings and a distinct fork in the longer tail. The plumage is a mixture of russet red and chestnut brown with white wing patches and a silver head. Their flight is more agile and a close view will show the tail constantly twisting as if trimming a sail.

Walk 19

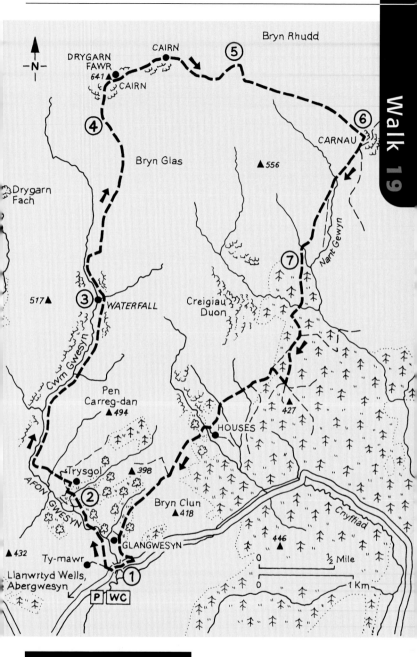

Walk 19 Directions

① Head up the gravel track west of the lay-by and turn right, through a gate. Follow the track across fields and down to the **Afon Gwesyn**, which you ford. Continue to a gate and up towards a wood where the track splits. Choose the top option and then, as this bends around to the left and heads downhill, fork right, to traverse the clearing to a gap in the wood.

② Follow the path down to a ford. Climb on to open ground and bear right to a farm track by some buildings. Turn left on to this and follow it through a gate and beneath some crags. Ignore a fork to the left and continue to open ground. Follow the east side of the valley for over 1½ miles (2.4km) to a **waterfall**.

③ Pass this on the right, then continue until the path almost disappears. Follow the line of the stream until you reach a distinctive small ridge coming in from the right. Take this for 100yds (91m) and bear left on to a narrow path, which leads you around a number of boggy patches until the cairned summit of **Drygarn Fawr** becomes visible ahead.

WHERE TO EAT AND DRINK ⓘ
The **Neuadd Arms** in Llanwrtyd Wells is a haven for walkers and an excellent pub with a good atmosphere, a glowing fire and tasty food. Dogs allowed in the bar.

④ Climb the grassy slope to the trig point, then follow the ridge east past both **cairns**. A close scan of the hillsides to the south east should reveal two grassy tops, 1½ miles (2.4km) away, one with a large cairn on top – this is **Carnau**, your next objective. A clear grassy track descends east from the cairn. Follow this until it levels completely and rounds a left-hand bend, where you'll make out a faint path forking right. This is the start of the careful navigation and if you're in any doubt about visibility, you'll be better off turning around and retracing your tracks.

⑤ Follow the track, which links a number of boundary stones for 200yds (183m), until you see one

stone offset to the right of the path. Turn sharp right here (south), away from the path, and cross wet ground to climb slightly on to a very broad rounded ridge. You'll make out the head of a small valley ahead and, as you drop into this, bear slightly left to follow the high ground with the valley to your right. Continue on sheep tracks to cross a couple of hollows, until you reach a grassy hilltop. From here, you should be able to see the cairn ahead. Take the clear path that leads to it.

⑥ From **Carnau** you'll see the start of a clear gorge away to the south west. Walk towards this and pick up a good track that leads across the river. Follow the bank to the left to reach a fork and then take the right-hand path to descend open hillsides and drop into the bottom of the valley, where it meets the wood.

⑦ Go through the gate and follow the forest track down across a stream and up to a five-way junction. Turn sharp right here, go through a gate and then another on the left. Drop down through the field on to an enclosed track and follow this to a junction above some houses on your left. Keep right, cross a stream and then take the track across a field to a path junction. Keep straight ahead and descend past **Glangwesyn** to the road. Turn right on to the road to return to your car.

WHILE YOU'RE THERE ⓘ
In winter, enquire in the Neuadd Arms in Llanwrtyd Wells for details of the **red kite feeding** which usually takes place at around 12:30PM near a hide on the outskirts of the village. It can be quite spectacular and will guarantee you a sighting of these wonderful birds.

Back to Nature

The formidable crags of one of the Beacon's best-known nature reserves.

Walk 20

•DISTANCE•	4 miles (6.4km)
•MINIMUM TIME•	2hrs
•ASCENT / GRADIENT•	1,050ft (320m) ▲▲▲
•LEVEL OF DIFFICULTY•	🚶🚶 🚶
•PATHS•	Clear footpaths and broad stony tracks, 4 stiles
•LANDSCAPE•	Imposing crags and rolling moorland, great views
•SUGGESTED MAP•	aqua3 OS Explorer OL12 Brecon Beacons National Park Western & Central areas
•START / FINISH•	Grid reference: SN 972221
•DOG FRIENDLINESS•	Difficult stiles, care near livestock, on lead in nature reserve
•PARKING•	Pull-in by small picnic area on A470, 2 miles (3.2km) north of Storey Arms
•PUBLIC TOILETS•	Storey Arms car park

BACKGROUND TO THE WALK

This is a short walk but it has much to offer. Firstly, there are some fine views over the Tarell Valley to the true kings of the National Park, Pen y Fan and Corn Du, whose lofty crowns command your attention for most of the way round. And secondly, the daunting crags of Craig Cerrig-gleisiad are a true spectacle in their own right and are well worth admiring close up, both from below and above.

This is a unique environment and, as such, it hosts a range of habitats that support a number of rare species of flora and fauna. The cirque itself was formed by the action of an ice-age glacier, which scoured out a deep hollow in the hillside and then deposited the rocks it had accumulated at the foot of the cliff to form banks of moraine. The retreating ice left a legacy – a selection of arctic-alpine plants that were sheltered from the rising temperatures by the north-facing escarpment. These plants, which include saxifrages and roseroot, also need a lime-rich soil, present on the escarpments but not on the more acidic moorland on the tops. For most of these plants, the Brecon Beacons represent the southernmost part of their range.

The cliffs only make up a fraction of the 156-acre (63ha) National Nature Reserve. One of the things that makes Craig Cerrig-gleisiad – which means 'Blue-stone Rock' – special is the diversity of the terrain. The lower slopes are home to mixed woodland and flowers such as orchids and anemones, while the high ground supports heather and bilberry. You'll see plenty of sheep within the reserve, but grazing is controlled to ensure a variety of habitats. The diversity isn't just restricted to plants either – 16 species of butterfly have been recorded on the reserve and over 80 different types of birds, including the ring ouzel, or mountain blackbird as it's often known, and the peregrine falcon, which is definitely a bird of the cliffs.

This mainly upland region of the Brecon Beacons National Park is partitioned from the central Brecon Beacons by the deep slash of the Taf and Tarell valleys. The name Fforest Fawr, which means Great Forest, comes not from trees but from its one-time status as a royal hunting ground. The high ground is largely untracked and barren, but the north-facing escarpment, of which Craig Cerrig-gleisiad forms a part, is steep and impressive. As the land

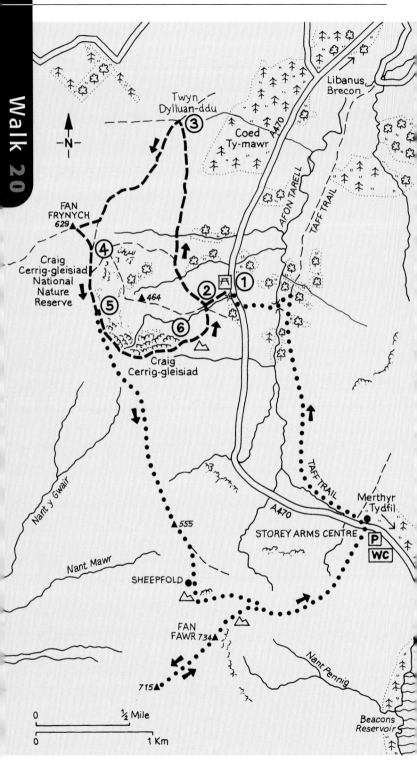

Twyn Dylluan-ddu

③

Libanus
Brecon

Coed
Ty-mawr

—N—

FAN
FRYNYCH
629

④

②

①

Craig
Cerrig-gleisiad
National
Nature
Reserve

▲*464*

⑤

⑥

Craig
Cerrig-gleisiad

AFON TARELL

TAFF TRAIL

Nant y Gwair

▲*555*

TAFF TRAIL

Merthyr
Tydfil

A470

STOREY ARMS CENTRE

P

WC

Nant Mawr

SHEEPFOLD

FAN
FAWR *734*▲

Nant Pennig

715▲

Beacons
Reservoir

0	½ Mile
0	1 Km

Walk 20

dips to the south, it is chiselled into a succession of north–south running valleys that cradle the infant forms of some of the National Park's greatest rivers. These are seen to best effect on the southern fringes of the park, where they form Fforest Fawr's greatest spectacle, Waterfall Country.

Walk 20 Directions

① There's a bridge and a small picnic area at the southern end of the lay-by. Walk towards this and go through the adjacent kissing gate (signposted to Twyn Dylluan-ddu and Forest Lodge). Head towards the crags, following a clear footpath, until you come to a gap in the next wall.

> **WHILE YOU'RE THERE** ⓘ
> This is the nearest walk to the **National Park Visitor Centre** on Mynydd Illtud Common, near Libanus. It's a great source of information about the National Park, hosts some great displays and has a programme of guided walks.

② Pass through this and turn right to follow a dry-stone wall north. Head down into a small valley, cross the stream, then a stile to continue in the same direction. Drop into another, steeper, valley and climb out, still following the track. Continue through the bracken to a stile.

③ Cross and turn left on to a stony track. Follow this up to a gate and a stile and continue through rough ground, churned up by mining, until it levels on a dished plateau. Bear right here to the whitewashed

trig point of **Fan Frynych**, then turn sharp left to return to the main track above the escarpment.

④ Turn right on to the main track again and continue past more rough ground before dropping slightly into a broad but shallow valley. At the bottom, go over a stile by a gate.

⑤ Cross another stile on your left and turn right to continue in the same direction, this time with the fence to your right. Climb up to the highest point, then follow the obvious path around the top of the cliffs. The path starts to drop, easily at first but getting steeper as you go.

> **WHERE TO EAT AND DRINK** ⓘ
> The **National Park Visitor Centre** at Libanus serves tasty lunches, with vegetarian options, as well as delicious home-made cakes. If you fancy a pub there's the **Tai'r Bull Inn**, also at Libanus.

⑥ Continue carefully down the steep section and follow the path around to the left when you reach easier ground. This leads you to a stream, which you can ford or jump (it's narrower a few paces downstream). Turn right, through the gap in the wall, and follow the outward path back to the car park.

> **WHAT TO LOOK FOR** ⓘ
> Much of the outward leg follows the line of a pristine **dry-stone wall**. Although changes in farming practices in the hills haven't altered as radically as they have in many lowland areas, the hedgerows and walls that once divided the land are expensive to maintain and have been slowly replaced by wire fences. The National Park Authority provides free consultation to landowners wishing to keep the more scenic traditional crafts alive.

Regenerating Bourton-on-the-Water

A walk on the wilder side of bustling Bourton-on-the-Water to see the results of its natural regeneration.

•DISTANCE•	4¾ miles (7.7km)
•MINIMUM TIME•	2hrs
•ASCENT / GRADIENT•	230ft (70m)
•LEVEL OF DIFFICULTY•	
•PATHS•	Track and field, can be muddy and wet in places, 26 stiles
•LANDSCAPE•	Sweeping valley views, lakes, streams, hills and village
•SUGGESTED MAP•	aqua3 OS Outdoor Leisure 45 The Cotswolds
•START / FINISH•	Grid reference: SP 169208
•DOG FRIENDLINESS•	Some stiles may be awkward for dogs; occasional livestock
•PARKING•	Pay-and-display car park on Station Road
•PUBLIC TOILETS•	At car park

BACKGROUND TO THE WALK

Despite Bourton-on-the-Water's popularity the throng is easily left behind by walking briefly eastwards to a chain of redundant gravel pits. In the 1970s these were landscaped and filled with water and fish. As is the way of these things, for some time the resulting lakes looked every inch the artificial creations they were, but now they have bedded into their surroundings and seem to be an integral part of the landscape.

Migrating Birds

The fish and water have acted as magnets for a range of wetland birds, whose populations rise and fall with the seasons. During the spring and summer months you should look out for the little grebe and the splendidly adorned great crested grebe, as well as the more familiar moorhens and coots, and mallard and tufted ducks. Wagtails will strut about the water's edge, swans and geese prowl across the water and kingfishers, if you are lucky, streak from bush to reed. Come the autumn, the number of birds will have increased significantly. Above all there will be vast numbers of ducks – pintail, shoveler, widgeon and pochard among them – as well as occasional visitors like cormorants. Either around the lakes or by the rivers you may also spy dippers and, in the hedgerows, members of the finch family.

Immigrant Birds

Should you get drawn into the village – as you surely will – keep listening for birdsong and you will hear some improbable 'visitors'. Bourton-on-the-Water has a large bird sanctuary which houses, among many other birds, one of the largest collections of penguins in the world, some of which featured in the film *Batman* (1989). A penguin seems an odd choice for an adversary, given its endearing reputation, and at first glance one might think that a penguin was a mammal and a bat was a bird, not vice versa. The reason for the presence of so many penguins in the Cotswolds is that the sanctuary's founder was also the owner of two small islands in the Falklands.

Walk 21

Long History

Penguins aside, Bourton-on-the-Water has a long history. The edge of the village is bounded by the Roman Fosse Way and many of its buildings are a pleasing mix of medieval, Georgian and Victorian. Although the village can become very crowded during the summer months, with the riverbanks at its centre like green beaches, strewn with people picnicking and paddling, it can still be charming. Arrive early enough in the morning, or hang around in the evening until the daytrippers have gone and you will find the series of bridges spanning the Windrush (one of which dates back to 1756) and the narrow streets beyond them highly picturesque. They retain the warm honeyed light that attracts people to the Cotswolds. You'll see far fewer visitors in little Clapton-on-the-Hill, which overlooks Bourton. Make the brief detour after Point ④ to see its handsome green and tiny church.

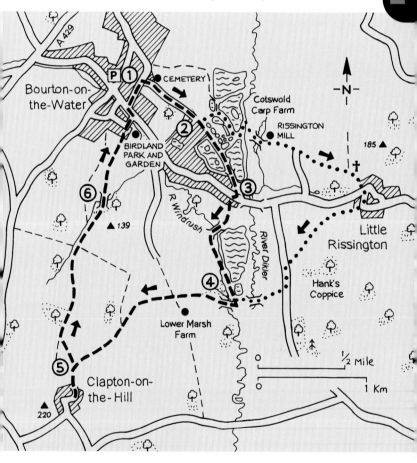

Walk 21 **Directions**

① Opposite the entrance to the main pay-and-display car park in **Bourton-on-the-Water** locate a public footpath and continue to a junction opposite the **cemetery**. Bear right to follow a lane all the way to its end. There are two gates in front of you. Take the one on the right, with a stile beside it, to enter a grassy track.

Walk 21

② Follow the track between lakes to where it curves right. Leave the track to go forward over a bridge and stile into a field. Go across the field, curving right, to come to a stile at a road.

③ Cross the road, turn right and immediately left on to a track. After 100yds (91m) go left over a stile into a field and turn right. Cross a stile and return to the track, with a lake to your left. Just before a gate turn right over a bridge and left over a stile on to a path alongside the **River Windrush**. Continue until the path comes to a stile at a field. Turn left, cross another stile and go left over a bridge before turning right beside another lake.

> **WHAT TO LOOK FOR** ⓘ
> In the autumn, in particular, keep an eye out for **swans**. Mute swans – the most common type, with the orange bill – are present all the year round, but the whooper swan, with its erect neck and yellow bill, is only a winter visitor, flying in from northern Europe and Russia.

④ Where this second, smaller lake ends bear right to a stile, followed by a bridge and stile at a field. Keep to the right side of fields until you come to a track. At a house leave the track and continue to a stile. In the next field, after 25yds (23m), turn left over a stile and then sharp right. Continue to a stile and then go half left across a field. Continue

> **WHERE TO EAT AND DRINK** ⓘ
> There are no pubs in Clapton. Bourton-on-the-Water has many pubs, tea shops and restaurants, catering to most tastes. Try the **Kingsbridge Inn** by the River Windrush, or the **Mousetrap** on Lansdown for reliable pub food. The **Old Manse**, also close to the river, serves a good lunch and dinner.

> **WHILE YOU'RE THERE** ⓘ
> Unlike other Cotswold villages, Bourton-on-the-Water has many and diverse attractions jostling for the contents of your wallet. The pick of these are probably **Birdland Park and Gardens** (see Background to the Walk) with their penguins, and the **Cotswold Motor Museum**, which has lots of pre-1950s cars as well as a few novelty items to thrill children. The most popular activity is arguably just strolling around.

on the same line across the next field to a stile. Cross this and follow the right margin of a field, to climb slowly to a junction of tracks. Turn left to visit the village of **Clapton-on-the-Hill**, or turn right to continue.

⑤ Follow a track to a field. Go forward then half right to pass right of **woodland**. Continue to a stile, followed by two stiles together at a field. Go half left to a stile and then follow a succession of stiles, a stream appearing to the left.

⑥ Cross a bridge and then go half right across a field to a bridge. Continue to more stiles and then walk along a grassy track towards houses. Cross one more stile and follow a path to a road in **Bourton**. Walk ahead to cross the river and turn left, then right, to return to the start.

Wanderings at Wychwood

A gentle walk through rolling Oxfordshire farmland and a corner of an ancient forest.

•DISTANCE•	5¾ miles (9.2km)
•MINIMUM TIME•	2hrs 30min
•ASCENT / GRADIENT•	574ft (175m) ▲▲▲
•LEVEL OF DIFFICULTY•	🕴🕴 🕴🕴 🕴
•PATHS•	Field paths, quiet roads, woodland tracks, no stiles
•LANDSCAPE•	Gently rolling hills of arable farmland, ancient woods
•SUGGESTED MAP•	aqua3 OS Explorer 180 Oxford, Witney & Woodstock
•START / FINISH•	Grid reference: SP 318194
•DOG FRIENDLINESS•	Lead essential for road stretches, otherwise excellent
•PARKING•	On village street near phone box, Chilson
•PUBLIC TOILETS•	None on route

BACKGROUND TO THE WALK

The Wychwood takes its name from a local Saxon tribe, the Hwicce. At the time of the Norman conquest, Wychwood Forest was one of four royal hunting grounds in England, and covered most of western Oxfordshire. The leafy remains of this once magnificent demesne are now mostly confined to the hilltops that lie between Ascott-under-Wychwood, Charlbury, Ramsden and Leafield, and private land ownership means that access for walkers is sometimes frustratingly limited.

A National Nature Reserve

At its heart is a National Nature Reserve, which preserves some 360 species of wild flowers and ferns, including the elusive yellow star of Bethlehem and the bizarre toothwort, a parasitic plant that is found on the roots of some trees. This walk takes you through the edge of the old woodland, on a path that in spring is carpeted with vivid drifts of bluebells that stretch away under the trees as far as the eye can see. The rich variety of wild flowers means a corresponding abundance of butterflies, including peacock, tortoiseshell and orange tip.

The Shrinking Forest

By 1300 the once-flourishing 'forest' had been split into three sections: Woodstock, based around the royal hunting lodge first built there during the reign of Ethelred II; the area around Cornbury Park; and a section around Witney, where the Bishop of Winchester had built his palace. The forest continued to decline and, by 1857, only some 10 square miles (26sq km) were left to be removed from Forest Law by an act of parliament. As the enclosure of land became commonplace in the 1860s, Kingstanding Farm, passed on this walk, was one of seven new farms built at this time to take advantage of the newly available land.

The Ascott Martyrs

The village of Ascott-under-Wychwood is tucked in the valley below the remnants of the Wychwood, along with its near-neighbours Shipton-under-Wychwood and Milton-under-

Wychwood. Ascott may not be the prettiest of these Cotswold villages, but it has another claim to fame: the Ascott Martyrs. These 16 young women played their part in the Agricultural Revolution of the 19th century when, in 1873, they attempted to dissuade Ramsden men from taking over the jobs of local men, who had been sacked for membership of the Agricultural Workers' Union. Indeed, the women were accused of encouraging the imported labourers to join the same union. Their punishment – imprisonment with hard labour – caused a riot outside the court in Chipping Norton and the women had to be secretly transferred to Oxford gaol. Their sentences were later remitted by Queen Victoria and some accounts say she sent each woman a red flannel petticoat and five shillings. The union presented them with blue silk for dresses and £5 each. These bold women are remembered with a bench on the village green.

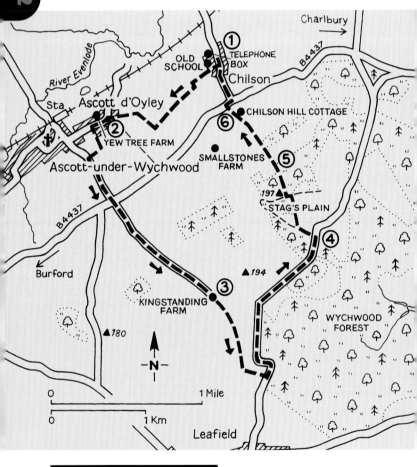

Walk 22 Directions

① From the phone box, turn south along the village street, and right up **School Lane**, passing various houses and the **Old School** at the end, on the right. Follow the path straight on into the field ahead, with the hedge to your right. Stay on the path round the edge of the field as it kinks left then right. Keep straight on, descend steadily, and follow as the track bends right.

Walk 22

At the hedge turn right then immediately left through a gateway; take the track diagonally left across the field towards Ascott-under-Wychwood, to meet a lane.

② Turn left along the lane through **Ascott d'Oyley**, passing **Yew Tree Farmhouse** on the right. Beyond d'Oyley House and just before a recreation ground turn left up a track, **Priory Lane**, which becomes a grassy path. This bends sharp right, and emerges at a road by a house. Turn left up the road, and cross the main road at the top with care. Continue straight ahead up the lane, signed 'Leafield'. Follow this straight uphill for a mile (1.6km), to pass through the buildings of **Kingstanding Farm**.

③ Continue down the stony track and keep straight on. It leads along the bottom of a winding, secret valley, with the solid spire of **Leafield church** up to your right. Emerge at a main road; turn left and follow the road as it snakes uphill, with **Wychwood Forest** to your right. After about 1 mile (1.6km) the road descends into woodland. As it ascends again, look for a wooden gate on the left, signed 'Circular Walk Footpath'.

④ Turn left through here and follow the path up the edge of the woods. Keep right and cross the

clearing of **Stag's Plain**. Bend left and right and continue on the path through the woods, carpeted with bluebells in spring.

⑤ Start to descend and emerge from the woods. Continue straight ahead, following the track downhill, with a hedge on your right. Pass **Smallstones Farm**, over to the left. Bend left at the bottom of the field, cross a stile, and take the path that leads to the left, down the hill and past **Chilson Hill Cottage** (right).

⑥ At the bottom of the drive turn right along the main road and immediately left down the road that leads into **Chilson** village. Enter the village and keep straight on past the tiny triangular green, passing the old **Primitive Methodist chapel** on your left. Pass the end of **School Lane** and return to your car.

Roaming Around Hanningfield Reservoir

Birds, wildlife, and a nature walk through meadows and woodlands.

•DISTANCE•	3½ miles (5.7km)
•MINIMUM TIME•	1hr 30min
•ASCENT / GRADIENT•	Negligible
•LEVEL OF DIFFICULTY•	
•PATHS•	Grassy and gravel forest tracks, prone to mud after rains, some boardwalk
•LANDSCAPE•	Reservoir, forest and grassy meadow
•SUGGESTED MAP•	aqua3 OS Explorer 175 Southend-on-Sea & Basildon
•START / FINISH•	Grid reference: TQ 725971
•DOG FRIENDLINESS•	No-go area except for guide dogs
•PARKING•	Free parking at the Visitor Centre, Hawkswood Road entrance. Gates close at 5PM
•PUBLIC TOILETS•	Visitor Centre

BACKGROUND TO THE WALK

If you're a birdwatcher, or just enjoy nature, then Hanningfield Reservoir and Nature Reserve is the place for you. The south eastern shores of the 970 acre (393ha) reservoir have been set aside as a nature reserve by the Essex Water Company and are a Site of Special Scientific Interest (SSSI). Managed by the Essex Wildlife Trust, it is best known for the prolific numbers of wintering and breeding wildfowl. Among them are nationally important numbers of coot, gadwall and tufted duck. If you're there in early winter you will also see pintails in large numbers. The chalk-based sludge on the western side of the reservoir supports plants uncommon in Essex, such as golden dock and marsh dock.

Pleasant Strolling

An interesting nature trail leads through the woodland, where there are several especially well-constructed bird hides overlooking the reservoir and banks enabling you to spend all day spotting species such as pochard, shoveler, shelduck and great crested grebe. But for non-twitchers, waymarked trails lead through ancient coppice and secondary woodland, with ponds, hedges and ditches. Pleasant strolls through four different woods, Chestnut, Peninsular, Well Wood and Hawkswood are there to be enjoyed.

Coppiced Woodland

Hanningfield Reservoir was built to provide water for an increased population after World War Two and, in the 1960s, the area which forms part of today's nature reserve, was planted with conifers. Thirty years later, in 1992, the Essex Wildlife Trust took over management of the site and the reserve is, today, renowned for its abundant wildlife. In Chestnut Wood there are areas of Scots pine which have been thinned to allow in light to the cleared sunny grasslands, which are an excellent habitat for butterflies and crickets. Ponds, ditches and piles of dead wood have attracted dragonflies, newts and grass snakes. In Peninsular Wood, near Point and Oak Hides, warblers nest and feed in an area which was cleared and allowed to regenerate as scrub. And in Well Wood and Hawkswood you can see the perimeters of ancient woodlands where coppiced hornbeams and hazel allow the old plant and animal communities to flourish once more.

Spend some time in the Visitor Centre, either before or after your nature walk, to see some novel conservation ideas in action, such as composting toilets which need no flush and a log-burning stove using wood from the reserve. Water is conserved by collecting rain water from a large roof and using it to top up two wildlife ponds beside the Visitor Centre. You can use complimentary binoculars (donation appreciated) to spot dozens of birds feeding at one of these ponds from the viewing gallery inside the centre.

Walk 23

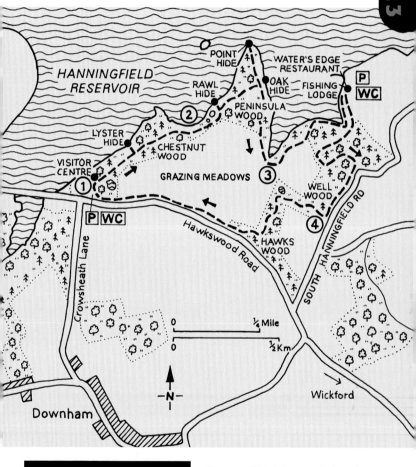

Walk 23 Directions

① From the **Visitor Centre**, take the path to **waymark C1** and detour left for views of the reservoir from **Lyster Hide**. Return to **C1** and continue along the path through

Chestnut Wood for 100yds (91m). At **waymark C2,** bear right towards the clearing and then go straight ahead towards tall oaks and **waymark C4.** Bear right here, over the wooden footbridge, passing the pond on your left, and continue until you reach **waymark C5** on the

Walk 23

edge of the wood. Ahead are grazing meadows. Turn left along the gravel path, keeping the meadow on your right, and follow the boardwalk to a clearing with deep water ponds and seating made from split trunks.

② Walk left past **waymark 7** to **Rawl Hide,** for good views of the reservoir and the reed covered embankment on the left. Now return to **waymark 7**, turn left on to the wide grassy path to enter **Peninsular Wood** and continue to **waymark 6**. Bear half left for 100yds (91m) and pass by Oak Hide to maintain direction to the tip of the peninsula and **waymark 5**, where you'll find **Point Hide**. Retrace your steps to **waymark 4** and walk ahead with the reservoir on your left. Maintain direction through thick forest passing **waymarks 3** and **2**, where you turn left and cross the bridge over the ditch.

③ Ignore the stile across to Hawkswood and turn left through thick forest for 200yds (183m) to **waymark B** and enter **Well Wood**. Turn left and then right for 200yds (183m) until you meet **waymark A**, with the **Fishing Lodge** and **Water's Edge** off to the left. Swing right and walk straight ahead, between coppiced trees with the high embankment on your left denoting the old boundary of the woods, to **waymark C**. Turn left, keeping meadows on your right, to **waymark D**. Turn left to **waymark K** and right to **waymark H**. Turn right again, into an area of less dense woodland with South Hanningfield Road on your left.

④ At **waymark F,** continue along the wide bridleway to a clearing of coppiced hornbeams. Descend timber steps, and past several small ponds to **waymark E** to enter **Hawkswood** passing **waymarks H1, H2** and **H3** in quick succession. At **H3** bear right over an earth bridge to **H10**, with meadow on your right, and bear left towards **H9** and **H11**. From here the path leads straight through hedgerows and a double set of kissing gates. Notice the pond on your right surrounded by a circle of chestnut trees and return to the car park.

Along the River Valley to Earls Colne

A fairly challenging walk along a disused railway track, now a nature reserve, and through ancient woodland.

•DISTANCE•	6½ miles (10.4km)
•MINIMUM TIME•	3hrs 30min
•ASCENT / GRADIENT•	78ft (24m) ▲ ▲ ▲
•LEVEL OF DIFFICULTY•	🚶 🚶 🚶
•PATHS•	Grassy with some muddy tracks, forest and field-edge paths, 3 stiles
•LANDSCAPE•	Disused railway line, ancient woodland, riverside and grazing meadows
•SUGGESTED MAP•	aqua3 OS Explorer 195 Braintree & Saffron Walden
•START / FINISH•	Grid reference: TL 855290
•DOG FRIENDLINESS•	Some stiles only suitable for chihuahuas, bigger dogs will need to be lifted
•PARKING•	Free parking at Queens Road car park in Earls Colne
•PUBLIC TOILETS•	Queens Road car park

BACKGROUND TO THE WALK

Is this the loveliest valley in all Essex? Judge for yourself as you follow the meandering River Colne and visit the delightful village of Earls Colne where the de Vere family, Earls of Oxford and one of the greatest families in English history, left their name. Here you will find a lovely view from the split-timber seating beside St Andrew's Church, with its tower visible for miles around; a nature reserve along a disused railway track, which has been cut back allowing wildlife to flourish, and the ancient woodlands of Chalkney Woods.

A Disused Railway Line

The Colne Valley Railway opened in 1860 and soon brought prosperity to the valley. Earls Colne, one of the stations on the line, was built by the Hunt family who developed the Atlas Works, which produced farming equipment until it closed in 1988. The line was used to import raw materials and to despatch the finished product, but since its closure in 1965 the track side vegetation has become a rich habitat for wildlife, with plenty of trees and shrubs providing heavy shade. As you walk along the disused track you will see evidence of coppicing which allows light to reach the ground, which in turn allows wildlife such as butterflies and other insects to proliferate.

Chalkney Wood dates back to 1605 when it was owned by the de Vere family. This walk takes you through the woods where conifers are gradually being replaced with traditional species to regenerate the woodland. You'll also see, near the kennels, an 18th-century watermill which last worked in the 1930s and is now a private residence. In the Alder Valley are the remains of conifer plantations established in the 1960s, but today the area supports more moss and liverworts than any other wood in East Anglia. You'll also pass close to the Wool Track, believed to be an ancient Roman road linking Colchester and Cambridge, and come across a prominent bank which enclosed the woods as a swine park where pigs would feed on acorns amongst the coppice.

Brickfields and Long Meadow Nature Reserve, bordered by woodland of oak, ash and hawthorn, has plenty of boggy areas and wet grassland. It is small, but has plenty of insect life. The ponds, surrounded by acacia and rhododendron, are home to newts, frogs and dragonflies. A major feature of the area is the anthills, which house huge colonies of yellow ants. Long Meadow, used for grazing, is free of fertilisers and pesticides, and as a result supports plenty of wildlife and a variety of grasses such as yarrow and birds trefoil. Near by you should also find a rare surviving elm tree.

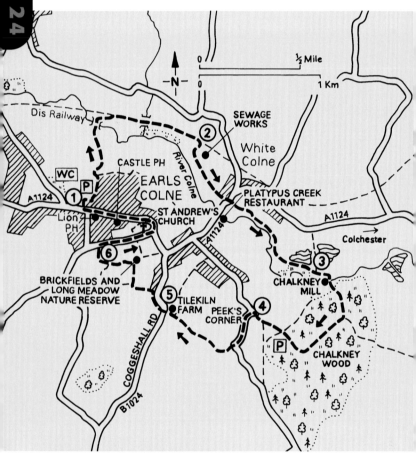

Walk 24 Directions

① From the car park, turn left and left again into **Burrows Road**. Cross **Hilly Bunnies Road** and maintain direction to the **Wildside waymark**. Here bear slightly right, then left on to the cross-field path, downhill across the golf course. Cross the footbridge following the yellow waymark over the **River Colne**. Follow the path for 70yds (64m) and bear left on the lesser path towards trees to the waymarked stile and information board marking the entrance to the railway nature reserve. Turn right on to the

Walk 24

railway embankment and maintain direction keeping the river and golf course on your right. Cross the footbridge over the **River Peb** and maintain your direction for about 600yds (549m).

② Leave the reserve by turning right at a collection of waymarks. Keep the fence of the sewage works on your left and follow the grassy path to reach **Colne Ford Road**. Turn left, cross the road, and follow the footpath and waymark between house Nos 20 and 22 through the wooden gate. Maintain direction across the meadow with the **River Colne** down on your right until you climb stile No 2.

> **WHERE TO EAT AND DRINK** ℹ️
>
> A good selection of eateries can be found in the High Street. Choose from the **Colne Valley Tandoori** restaurant which serves an 'eat-as-much-as-you-like' buffet on Sunday evenings or relax with your tired dog in the garden of the **Castle** pub. In Colneford Road you can enjoy a meal and drink at the **Platypus Creek** restaurant by the River Colne.

③ Turn right and cross the bridge over the Colne, passing kennels and **Chalkney Mill** on your right, and maintain direction into **Chalkney Wood**. Walk for 300yds (274m), take the second path on your right and go along the straight bridleway, bounded on the left by Corsican pine. Maintain direction for 500yds (457m) and bear right to the parking area. Take the wide downhill track for 300yds (274m) and turn left into **Tey Road** at **Peek's Corner**.

④ After 300yds (274m) turn right at the fingerpost and go along the field-edge path keeping the hedgerows on your right. Cross the

> **WHAT TO LOOK FOR** ℹ️
>
> The de Veres were great crusaders and were associated with a legendary silver star which was won outside the walls of Antioch on their first crusade. The family left their mark in the form of a star on buildings in this area of Essex, leaving no one in any doubt as to who owned and constructed them. One of these buildings is the unique star-studded tower of **St Andrew's Church**.

earth bridge through trees, maintain direction uphill, and pass Tilekiln Farm, on your right, to **Coggeshall Road**.

⑤ Turn right at Coggeshall Road and after 200yds (183m) turn left at the fingerpost marked **Park Lane**. Follow the path through the kissing gate and turn immediately right along the path bounded by thick gorse bushes. Follow the path left and downhill, keeping woods on your right, until you reach the **Wildside** waymarked stile. Cross the stile and walk along the field-edge path, keeping the hedgerow on your right, to an earth bridge where you turn right over the stream.

⑥ Take the path past a Brickfields information board on your right and turn right into **Park Lane** with St Andrews Church on your left. Turn left into **Coggeshall Road** and the **High Street** and return to the car park.

> **WHILE YOU'RE THERE** ℹ️
>
> If you're driving, head up to the **East Anglian Railway Museum** at Chappel Station to view a fine collection of goods and passenger rolling stock. Railway enthusiasts and children alike will love the interactive signal boxes and video displays in this working museum which covers a century of railway engineering in East Anglia.

Walk 25

Waltzing Around Walton-on-the-Naze

A day beside the Essex coast exploring a town with two seasides.

•DISTANCE•	4¼ miles (6.8km)
•MINIMUM TIME•	2hrs
•ASCENT / GRADIENT•	Negligible
•LEVEL OF DIFFICULTY•	
•PATHS•	Grassy cliff paths, tidal salt marsh and some town streets
•LANDSCAPE•	Cliffs, sandy beaches, creeks and marshes
•SUGGESTED MAP•	aqua3 OS Explorer 184 Colchester, Harwich & Clacton-on-Sea
•START / FINISH•	Grid reference: TM 253218
•DOG FRIENDLINESS•	The ozone drives dogs a little mad so take care on narrow paths along cliffs
•PARKING•	Pay-and-display at Mill Lane and Naze Tower
•PUBLIC TOILETS•	Mill Lane and Naze Tower

BACKGROUND TO THE WALK

In the early 19th century Walton-le-Soken, as Walton-on-the-Naze was then known, emerged as a seaside resort attracting fashionable folk from London and county families from Essex, who used bathing machines to dip their toes in the waters. The first terraced houses brought genteel residents, a hotel provided visitors with accommodation and before long the area became as popular as Southend with a pier packed with pastimes. Although Walton's name has since changed, two neighbouring villages, Kirby-le-Soken and Thorpe-le-Soken, still retain the original suffix.

Holiday Resort and Wildlife Haven

Nowadays visitors can enjoy amusement arcades, tenpin bowling, restaurants and sea fishing, and the holiday atmosphere is complete with kiss-me-quick hats, jellied eels and seaside rock. But if you wander north of the town and its lovely wide sandy beaches, you'll discover a haven for bird life in the John Weston Nature Reserve, named after a local warden, and a multitude of sailing craft tucked in the creeks.

Under Threat from Erosion

Part of the town is situated on a headland called The Naze, hence its name. The word originates from the Anglo-Saxon 'ness' or 'naes' meaning a headland, while Walton may mean 'walled town' from the sea wall. Natural erosion has played a big part in the development of Walton-on-the-Naze, although some would class it as terrifying destruction. In 1798 Walton's second church was washed away and at low tide they say you can still hear the bell ring; in 1880 its first pier was destroyed by heavy seas; World War Two gun emplacements and pillboxes built on the Naze itself fell on to the beach and in the next few years, the Naze Tower, a Grade II listed building, which is only just 100yds (91m) from the cliff edge will also be at risk.

Conservationists predict that unless coastal erosion is stopped, or at least slowed down to managable levels, then the area known as the Walton backwaters and home to thousands of birds, seals and other wildlife, will disappear along with a large part of Walton itself. It may come as no surprise that even the lifeboat here lacks a permanent mooring. In fact it is the only lifeboat in Britain to have a mooring in the open sea. It is near the end of the pier and, when the alarm is raised, the lifeboat crew cycle the length of the pier and use a small launch to reach it.

Choose a summer's day for this gentle walk, which takes you through the town and along the seafront to the Naze Tower. You can walk along the beach or along the promenade depending on the tidal conditions. Year round, Walton-on-the-Naze is a delight to explore. In winter you'll see waders and a range of wildfowl, including brent geese and, in summer, you may be lucky to spot rare avocets, which breed here. They have unusual upturned bills which they sweep through the water collecting shrimps and worms.

Walk 25

Walk 25

Walk 25 **Directions**

① From **Mill Lane car park** turn right into the **High Street** then left into **Martello Street**. Bear left along **New Pier Street** and go on to **Pier Approach**. To your right is the Pier, its ½ mile (800m) length makes it the second longest in England, after Southend. From here there are good views of the beaches of Walton-on-the-Naze and Frinton.

> **WHAT TO LOOK FOR** ⓘ
> You can see the **geological structure** of the cliffs from small promontories or from the beach. At the top of the cliffs the boulder clay and gravel date from the Ice Age. Below are red crag and the slippery grey deposits of London clay, which at the bottom look like brown flakes. Sand martins nest here.

② Turn left and, with the sea on your right, walk along **Princes Esplanade** through **East Terrace** at the end of which is the **Maritime Museum**. Continue walking along **Cliff Parade** and the cliff tops to **Naze Tower**. Built by Trinity House in 1720 as a navigational aid, it was to join many Martello towers which were constructed along the east and south east coasts of England to fend off Napoleonic invasion. Nowadays, the grassy area in which the tower stands is a good place to rest and recuperate with a hot drink and a picnic at the wooden tables.

> **WHILE YOU'RE THERE** ⓘ
> Call in at the **Maritime Museum** and see the exhibits relating to Frinton and Walton's close association with the sea and farming. This former lifeboat house also has displays on lifeboat history, including snippets on how the local lifeboat was regularly called out to pirate radio ships in distress in the 1960s.

③ From the car park café walk inland to **Old Hall Lane**, turn left and then right into **Naze Park Road**. At the end of Naze Park Road, where it bears sharp left, turn right on to the narrow path and left on to the field-edge path passing two small ponds filled with wildlife.

④ After 100yds (91m), turn left on to the cross path, go through the gate and on to the permissive path which follows the sea wall, keeping the caravan site on your left and **Walton Channel** on your right. This wide expanse of mudflats, islands, channels and small boats, ever changing with the tide, is a paradise for seabirds and a Site of Special Scientific Interest (SSSI). Skippers Island, an Essex Wildlife Trust nature reserve, is the habitat of rare seabirds and wildlife and full-time wardens are employed to protect them. Follow the sea wall for ¾ mile (1.2km) then bear half left down the embankment and into the field.

⑤ Walk 70yds (64m) to a path between the primary school playing field and houses and enter **Saville Street** past a row of old cottages on your right. Take the first right into **North Street**, continue to the **High Street** and turn right. Turn right again into **Mill Lane** and return to the car park.

> **WHERE TO EAT AND DRINK** ⓘ
> There are lots of cafés, fast food and fish and chip shops along the Esplanade and in the High Street. Open year round is **Grandma's** in Newgate Street, a delightful low-ceilinged restaurant offering steak and kidney pie and other treats. The **Victory** pub is next door while **White's** offers pie and mash and jellied or stewed eels. A snack bar beside Naze Tower keeps hungry walkers happy too.

The King's Wood at Wyre

A gorgeous leafy walk around Kingswood and Buttonoak in Wyre Forest.

•DISTANCE•	5 miles (8km)
•MINIMUM TIME•	2hrs 30min
•ASCENT / GRADIENT•	575ft (175m)
•LEVEL OF DIFFICULTY•	
•PATHS•	Woodland and field paths, 2 stiles
•LANDSCAPE•	Mostly broadleaved woodland, with some conifers
•SUGGESTED MAP•	aqua3 OS Explorer 218 Wyre Forest & Kidderminster
•START / FINISH•	Grid reference: SO 743784
•DOG FRIENDLINESS•	On lead in Longdon Orchard and on path to Kingswood
•PARKING•	Forestry Commission car park at Earnwood Copse, on south side of B4194, west of Buttonoak
•PUBLIC TOILETS•	None on route

BACKGROUND TO THE WALK

Wyre Forest is shared between Shropshire and Worcestershire, with Dowles Brook forming the county boundary. It was once a royal hunting forest, but the place name Kingswood is the only obvious reminder of that today. In the days of the Norman kings, the forest stretched from Worcester to Bridgnorth. It's considerably smaller today, and partially afforested with alien conifers, but it remains one of the largest and finest semi-natural woodlands in the country.

The Mighty Oak

Despite the conifers, there is still lots of broadleaved woodland, including species such as beech, silver birch, rowan, holly and hazel. But English oak is overwhelmingly dominant. There are two types of English oak – common (also known as pedunculate) and sessile (sometimes called durmast). Common oak usually dominates in the Midlands, but not in Wyre Forest, where the sessile oak is king. The underlying coal measures mean that much of the forest soil is acidic, the preferred habitat of the sessile oak.

English oak supports more wildlife than any other British tree, including an impressive 284 insect species. For centuries local people were also dependent on oak, which provided timber for houses, ships, pit props, fencing and a multitude of other uses. Small timber was used by broom makers and basket weavers, and also served as firewood. Oak twigs were bound together in bundles and used to make tracks suitable for horse-drawn carts, while oak bark, rich in tannin, was used for curing leather in the local tanneries. The forest is dotted with hamlets, such as Buttonoak, which grew out of woodland clearings known as assarts, where squatters settled illegally to make a living as basket weavers, broom makers or charcoal burners. The latter were known locally as wood colliers.

Walk here in autumn and you will see squirrels and jays everywhere, busily burying acorns for the winter. Some will be retrieved in due course, but those forgotten will germinate in spring to launch a new generation of oak trees. Unless, that is, the saplings are eaten by deer. Fallow deer are very common in Wyre and I have never walked in the forest without seeing several. Go quietly, with your dog on a lead, and you should see some too.

Walk 26 Directions

① Walk through a gate on to a forest road and immediately turn right on a footpath (no signpost or waymarker) into **Earnwood Copse**. Keep straight on at all junctions, eventually joining a sunken path not far from the edge of the forest. If you shortly pass under an overhanging yew tree you will know that you're on the right path (not that you're likely to go wrong, but forestry operations can sometimes bring about slight changes to the path network).

WHERE TO EAT AND DRINK ⓘ

The **Button Oak** is on the main road at Buttonoak. It's a friendly place, well used to welcoming walkers, including children. Dogs are welcome too, but not in the bar when food is being served. There's a pleasant beer garden outside.

---

② The path descends to meet what looks like a firebreak but is actually the route of the Elan Valley pipeline, bringing Welsh water to Birmingham. Turn right here and cross a footbridge on the edge of the forest, to the right of the pipeline. Walk up a bank into arable fields and then follow a waymarked field-edge footpath uphill. When you reach the top, go through a hedge gap and turn left towards the hamlet of **Kingswood**.

③ Soon after passing a sensitively restored timber-framed cottage (**Manor Holding**), you come to a T-junction at the edge of the forest. Go a few paces to the left towards **Kingswood Farm** and then you'll see a track that swings right to enter the forest. Keep straight on at all junctions, walking through **Brand Wood**.

④ You'll soon reach **Dowles Brook**. Don't cross; turn left on a bridleway that runs beside it. Follow the bridleway for 1¼ miles (2km), with **Wimperhill Wood** on your left.

⑤ Turn left on another bridleway, which first passes through a marshy area, then climbs through scrub and young woodland. It's waymarked and easily followed. After crossing a forest road, go straight on, but turn right at the next waymarked junction before swinging left to resume your original heading. After crossing a stream, the bridleway turns right as it climbs above the rim of a steep valley.

⑥ Turn sharp left (still on the bridleway) through a gap between two fenced areas, where birch and other natives are regenerating fast following clear felling of the conifers that grew here. You're approaching **Longdon Orchard** now, a conservation area where your dog must be under strict control. At the next junction go left, into conifers, then soon turn right.

⑦ Turn right when you meet the Elan Valley pipeline again, then very soon left, still on the bridleway. Follow it up to the edge of the forest near **Buttonoak**, then turn left to return to **Earnwood Copse**.

WHILE YOU'RE THERE ⓘ

Bewdley is in Worcestershire and it's well worth a visit. Once a busy Severn port, it now caters for tourists instead of boat builders and bow-hauliers (the men who pulled the boats upstream before somebody invented towing horses). Bewdley's waterfront is said to be the finest in the Midlands, and anybody who appreciates 17th- and 18th-century architecture will love this little town.

Here be Dragons

Explore Merrington's medieval common and a sandstone ridge at Webscott.

•DISTANCE•	5½ miles (8.8km)
•MINIMUM TIME•	2hrs 15min
•ASCENT / GRADIENT•	344ft (105m) ▲ ▲ ▲
•LEVEL OF DIFFICULTY•	🚶 🚶 🚶
•PATHS•	Field paths and bridleway, can be muddy, 6 stiles
•LANDSCAPE•	Farmland, medieval common, sandstone ridge with reclaimed quarries, panoramic views
•SUGGESTED MAP•	aqua3 OS Explorer 241 Shrewsbury
•START / FINISH•	Grid reference: SJ 465208
•DOG FRIENDLINESS•	Under control at Myddle, Merrington and Webscott
•PARKING•	Car park on north side of road at Merrington Green nature reserve
•PUBLIC TOILETS•	None on route

BACKGROUND TO THE WALK

The two main highlights of this walk are the former quarries at Webscott and the nature reserve managed by Shropshire Wildlife Trust at Merrington Green. It's a story of contrast. Webscott is a relatively new landscape, created by nature taking over a post-industrial site. Since quarrying ceased here, the holes so crudely gouged out of the sandstone have been colonised by mosses, ferns and trees. The effect is delightful. Merrington Green, on the other hand, is a very old landscape which can be maintained only by human management, otherwise nature will turn it into just another woodland.

Of course, it would have been woodland originally, but in the Middle Ages it was cleared. At that time, nearly every village would have had a similar patch of land where commoners could graze stock, collect firewood and dig marl or turf. Such a system results in a range of habitats, which is often more ecologically valuable than a uniform block of woodland. Merrington Green is still a registered common, but the commoners no longer exercise their rights, which means scrub is encroaching. It is controlled by hand as far as possible, but the reintroduction of grazing would be a better way. However, sheep would be at risk from traffic because the green is unfenced.

Spectacular Aerobatics

One of the most valuable aspects of the green is the presence of three pools which have formed in old marl pits. An incredible 17 species of dragonfly and damselfly have been recorded here, making this easily Shropshire Wildlife Trust's top dragonfly location. The easternmost pool is fringed by marsh horsetail, a descendant of the giant horsetails of the primeval swamps, where the first dragonflies evolved over 300 million years ago. The largest species of dragonfly ever known is preserved in the fossil record from this time – it had a wingspan the size of a sparrowhawk's. Modern dragonflies are much smaller and each is a miniature miracle of design. If you get to see a resting dragonfly it's worth studying it in detail to appreciate the lethal beauty of these precision-built killing machines. Typically, an adult dragonfly will live only a few weeks, but in that time it will consume large numbers of smaller insects, caught on the wing. Its aerial acrobatics can be spectacular and its wings beat 30 times a second, allowing a dazzling range of manoeuvres. It can even fly backwards. The adult stage is preceded by two or three years spent under water as a nymph, in which form the insect is also a consummate predator. When a nymph is ready to metamorphose, it climbs out of the water on to a suitable plant. The ugly larval skin splits and a jewel-coloured adult emerges, crumpled at first, until it dries off and its wings inflate.

Walk 27

Walk 27 **Directions**

① There is a map of the reserve on one side of the car park and, on the other side, two footpaths: you can

take either as they soon merge into one. Follow the path through grassland, then fork left into woodland. Turn right when you meet a pool. After passing one side of the pool, the path moves briefly

Walk 27

away from it, then turns left to pass the end of it, with another pool on your right-hand side and a boardwalk underfoot.

② Turn left on a tree-bordered bridleway, which runs for nearly 2 miles (3.2km). As you approach a road, look for a stile on the right (at a bend) and walk across fields to meet the road on the edge of **Myddle**. Turn right into the village.

> **WHILE YOU'RE THERE** ⓘ
> In 1403, Henry IV defeated the Yorkists at the Battle of Shrewsbury. The site is simply called **Battlefield**, and there's a church there, just to the north of Shrewsbury. It was built on the King's orders after the battle, and eight chaplains were installed to pray for the dead. It's very atmospheric, even when the church itself is closed.

③ After passing the **church**, turn right on a walled lane, then through a black gate on the left. Pass to the left of farm buildings, then cross two fields – you can see the path stretching ahead of you to a lane.

④ Turn right along the lane for 400yds (366m) until you can join a footpath on the left, which climbs a wooded slope. At the top a well-trodden path turns right by the woodland edge. However, the right of way goes diagonally across a field to a gate to the road.

⑤ Turn your back on the gate and go straight across the field, meeting the wood again at a corner. Go through a gate and descend through the trees, then through a garden (dogs on leads) and past a cottage towards the lane. Just before you reach it, join another path on the left that climbs back up the slope. As you approach a stile at the top,

> **WHERE TO EAT AND DRINK** ⓘ
> Try the **Red Castle** or the **Bridgewater Arms**, or the exceptionally good organic café and farm shop at **Lea Hall** (no dogs allowed), all on the A528 at nearby Harmer Hill.

turn right, then left, descending through a former **quarry** and past a lovely house built into the rock. Turn right along the lane.

⑥ Join a footpath on the left and cross a narrow pasture. A right of way runs diagonally across the next field, but is currently impassable at the far side. If you suspect this may still be the case (new waymarkers might indicate improvements), play safe by taking another path, which follows the right-hand field edge.

⑦ Turn left along **Merrington Lane**, and eventually right at a T-junction at **Merrington**. When the road bends left, go straight on along the bridleway used earlier until you join a path that crosses the nature reserve to the car park.

> **WHAT TO LOOK FOR** ⓘ
> You will notice some footpaths have waymarkers labelled '**Gough walk**'. This is a millennium project, inspired by Richard Gough (1635–1723), who achieved fame through his book *The Antiquities and Memoirs of the Parish of Myddle*. Go in the church to find out more – it's fascinating stuff, and you can buy a pack of walk leaflets if you wish.

Woodgate Valley Country Park

A short, easy excursion showing the West Midlands' urban countryside at its best.

•DISTANCE•	3½ miles (5.7km)
•MINIMUM TIME•	1hr 30min
•ASCENT / GRADIENT•	49ft (15m)
•LEVEL OF DIFFICULTY•	
•PATHS•	Grassy footpaths and tracks, 2 stiles
•LANDSCAPE•	Country park
•SUGGESTED MAP•	aqua3 OS Explorers 219 Wolverhampton & Dudley; 220 Birmingham
•START / FINISH•	Grid reference: SP 995829 (on Explorer 219)
•DOG FRIENDLINESS•	Off lead around park
•PARKING•	Woodgate Valley Country Park
•PUBLIC TOILETS•	Country Park visitor centre building

BACKGROUND TO THE WALK

Birmingham is surrounded by country parks, which act as the lungs of the city. Woodgate Valley Country Park is one of these vital green spaces and this walk takes you past an urban farm complex and along the side of the babbling Bourn Brook, which runs the length of the valley to the River Rea at Cannon Hill Park.

Woodgate Valley Country Park

The park comprises some 450 acres (182ha) of meadows, hedgerows and woodland on the western edge of Birmingham. It was originally a mixture of farms and smallholdings and every effort has been made to retain its rural appeal. Threatened by development, it was designated a Country Park in 1984. A programme of hedge and tree replanting has taken place and the visitor centre opened in 1987.

The woodland, ponds and meadows have now become home to a vast range of wildlife and hundreds of species of plants and flowers. Hawthorn, hazel, honeysuckle and ivy all thrive and, in the spring, bluebells and foxgloves add a blanket of colour. The meadowlands near the start of this walk, known as Pinewoods, are a treat to stroll through on a warm summer's day. Pheasants, kingfishers, cuckoos, chiffchaffs, whitethroats and willow warblers are regular visitors, and, if you're lucky, you may see a long-eared owl or even a marsh harrier. When the plants are in flower, butterflies arrive in large numbers and some 20 species have been seen during a normal summer. Look out especially for the red admiral and the small tortoiseshell.

During 2001, the foot and mouth epidemic resulted in the closure of many footpaths in the Midlands countryside and Woodgate Valley Park became a refuge for walkers and ramblers from outlying areas. Although it is close to so many urban roads, you can enjoy peace and tranquillity away from the noise. It is surrounded by houses, yet very few can be seen when you are walking the footpaths along the side of Bourn Brook.

Underground Canal

Beneath the parkland are the remains of part of the Lapal Tunnel on the Dudley No 2 Canal, which connected Halesowen with Selly Oak. It is one of the longest canal tunnels in England and a reminder that the industrial side of Birmingham is never too far away, even if you can't actually see it. The canal was built in 1790 despite fierce local opposition as industrial expansion in the West Midlands was proceeding at a frightening pace. Measuring only 9ft (2.7m) wide and 9ft (2.7m) from water level to ceiling, it gradually fell into disuse with competition from the railways. Following mining subsidence in 1917, the tunnel was closed and finally sealed off in 1926, though there is an active campaign to reopen it sometime in the future.

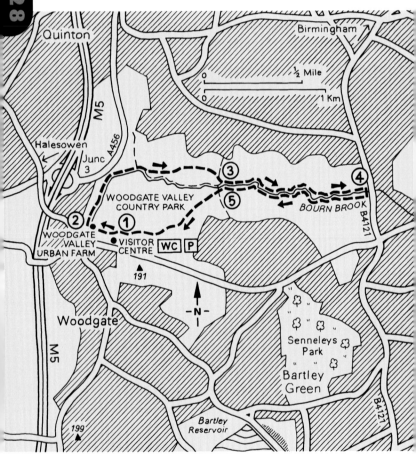

Walk 28 **Directions**

① Walk from the car park down to the **Woodgate Valley Urban Farm**. Go left past the animal enclosures and follow the waymarker signed 'Footpaths and Bridlepaths'.

② When you reach the lane, go right along the tarmac footpath by the side of a stream – the **Bourn Brook** – with the bridlepath up to the left. This path arcs right, around the edge of the park until you reach a footbridge over the brook. At the footbridge, bear left past the large

Walk 28

oak tree and a bench seat and walk along a footpath that arcs away from the stream towards an area of young trees. This is easy, pleasant walking and in about 150yds (137m) you will come to a junction of footpaths. Continue left ahead (if you go right you will return to the Bourn Brook), keeping to the right of the young trees as you progress in a generally easterly direction on the grass path that meanders along the edge of the trees.

③ Another footpath comes in from the left and then, at a junction of footpaths, bear right towards a rather high footbridge over the stream. Do not cross it, instead bear left and follow the footpath on the left side of Bourn Brook. This leads into the trees and there follows a very pleasant stroll through the park, always close to the bank of the stream.

④ All too soon you will hear the noise of traffic on the B4121 ahead. Just before you reach the road, go right over the footbridge and follow the footpath down the other side of the stream. The path passes close to housing, but this is barely visible and the country feel is maintained until you reach the high footbridge once again.

⑤ Do not go over the footbridge but leave the Bourn Brook behind and bear left to take a footpath that crosses open land diagonally with houses to your left (do not go left towards the houses). Maintain your direction over a second open area, passing close to a hedgerow of blackberry bushes. At the end, bear right on to the main tracks passing by a football pitch to arrive back at the visitor centre.

Where the Wild Things Are – a Sutton Park Experience

A longer walk visiting the largest National Nature Reserve in the West Midlands.

•DISTANCE•	7¼ miles (11.7km)
•MINIMUM TIME•	2hrs 30min
•ASCENT / GRADIENT•	230ft (70m) ▲▲▲
•LEVEL OF DIFFICULTY•	🚶 🚶 🚶
•PATHS•	Footpaths, tracks and road in parkland
•LANDSCAPE•	Undulating parkland
•SUGGESTED MAP•	aqua3 OS Explorer 220 Birmingham
•START / FINISH•	Grid reference: SP 112961
•DOG FRIENDLINESS•	Off lead in park
•PARKING•	Visitor centre car park, Sutton Park
•PUBLIC TOILETS•	Visitor centre, Sutton Park

BACKGROUND TO THE WALK

Sutton Park comprises 2,400 acres (970ha) of wild and wooded countryside of moorland, meadows, lakes and groves and is one of the largest urban parks in the country. The ancient Roman Ryknild Street runs across one corner of the park and the Normans once hunted deer here. Shakespeare had kinsmen at Sutton and is likely to have visited the site. One of his famous characters, Sir John Falstaff, probably brought his Ragged Army here for he declared to Bardolph:

> *'Get thee before to Coventry; fill me a bottle of sack; our soldiers shall march through. We'll to Sutton Coldfield tonight.'*
>
> William Shakespeare
> *King Henry IV, Part I*

Birmingham's Lung

In 1997, English Nature designated Sutton Park a National Nature Reserve (NNR) in an effort to preserve this wonderful landscape. Although it is now surrounded on all sides by residential properties it remains an important area for Birmingham and the local Sutton Coldfield community. It's a valuable space in an otherwise congested region and offers a wide range of leisure pursuits – for joggers, kite-fliers, cyclists and walkers. Despite all this activity, it is still possible to escape from the crowds and find peace and quiet.

It is the diversity of habitats in the park which earned its NNR status. Many areas, like the heathland, wetland and ancient forest, represent habitats which were once widespread but have now completely disappeared from the rest of the West Midlands. For this reason, it is the home of a large number of resident birds, as well as providing an important stop-over for migrants and other visitors. Around the pools you might see tufted duck, pochard and even snipe, especially near Longmoor Pool. It is hoped that red kites and other species, which have vanished from the region's skies, will one day return.

The nearby market town of Sutton Coldfield was important in the Middle Ages and owes a great deal to local benefactor John Veysey, who became bishop of Exeter in 1519. He lived at Moor Hall, now inside the famous park, and built a number of notable buildings in and around the town. He also founded a school and paved the streets. Veysey is buried in Holy Trinity Church and there is a fine effigy of him on his tomb. It depicts him as a young man, even though he is reputed to have lived to the ripe old age of 103. The church also contains some interesting old brasses. In particular there is one of a Josias Bull in a gown of fur, along with small brasses of his five children. The marble busts of Henry Pudsey and his wife were made by William Wilson, a mason for Sir Christopher Wren.

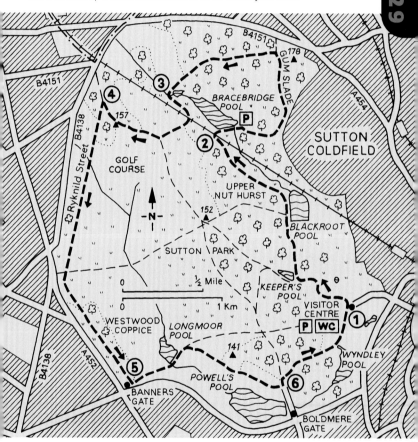

Walk 29 Directions

① Walk from the car park to the entrance road and go left up to **Keeper's Pool**. At the bottom of the pool, bear right through a gate and follow the edge of the pool, then go northwards through the trees on a path until you reach **Blackroot Pool**. Walk along the left edge of the pool for about 220yds (201m), then bear left (north west) and take the track through the woodland of **Upper Nut Hurst**. In about ½ mile (800m), turn right and cross the railway track to arrive at **Bracebridge Pool**.

Walk 29

② Turn right, along the edge of the pool, and at the end bear right along a track. Go through the car park and then left along the park road for about 100yds (91m) on to a track leading into the woodland of **Gum Slade**. Continue to a junction of paths, then go left across a grassy clearing. Proceed into the woodland on a track that arcs left and gently descends to cross a footbridge at the end of **Bracebridge Pool**.

③ Follow the track as it arcs left and then right to cross the railway line again. Continue along the track until you reach a road, then go right for 750yds (686m) up to a wide straight track.

> ### WHAT TO LOOK FOR ℹ️
> **Bracebridge Pool** is regarded by many people as the most beautiful pool in the park. It was built for Sir Ralph Bracebridge in order to maintain a plentiful supply of fish. In 1419, he obtained a lease on the manor and chase of Sutton Coldfield from the Earl of Warwick.

④ Head left and walk along this track for the next mile (1.6km). Cross the small brook and walk beside the golf course to a road exit from the park. Don't leave the park; instead cross the road and bear left along a pathway through the trees of **Westwood Coppice** until you come to the car park by **Banners Gate**.

⑤ Bear left up the road, passing to the right of **Longmoor Pool**. About 90yds (82m) beyond the end of the pool, head right along the track. After passing to the right of the trees, cross an open grass area close to **Powell's Pool** to reach the roadway near **Boldmere Gate**.

> ### WHERE TO EAT AND DRINK ℹ️
> There are a number of places in **Sutton Park** with cafés and kiosks at the various park entrances. Alternatively you could try one of the pubs in **Sutton Coldfield**, in particular along Chester Road North (the A452), just outside the park.

⑥ Go left along the road for 130yds (121m), then right, through the edge of **Wyndley Wood**. In 220yds (201m) bear right on to a straight road that leads to a cattle grid and ford at the end of **Wyndley Pool**. Continue ahead to return to the **visitor centre**.

> ### WHILE YOU'RE THERE ℹ️
> The **Wall Roman Site Baths and Museum** lies 9 miles (14.5km) north of Sutton Coldfield, near Lichfield. Here you will see the excavation of the most complete public bathhouse of a Roman staging post, known as Letocetum. It's situated just off Watling Street, the great arterial road that connected the Roman port at Richborough, near Canterbury, with London and the north west. Less than a mile (1.6km) away from Letocetum, Watling Street intersects the Icknield Way, running south west to north east, so this must have been a very important highway junction during the Roman era – a Spaghetti Junction of it's day, with the bathhouse at the heart of a motorway service area.

Birds and Bunnies at East Wretham Common

Once shaken by roaring Second World War aeroplanes, this is now a peaceful nature reserve.

Walk 30

•DISTANCE•	2¾ miles (4.4km)
•MINIMUM TIME•	1hr
•ASCENT / GRADIENT•	Negligible
•LEVEL OF DIFFICULTY•	
•PATHS•	Gravel track and way-marked trails across heath
•LANDSCAPE•	Heathland with some sparse pine plantations
•SUGGESTED MAP•	aqua3 OS Explorer 229 Thetford Forest in the Brecks
•START / FINISH•	Grid reference: TL 913885
•DOG FRIENDLINESS•	No dogs allowed in nature reserve
•PARKING•	Norfolk Wildlife Trust car park off A1075. Open 8AM to dusk
•PUBLIC TOILETS•	None on route

BACKGROUND TO THE WALK

When you arrive at East Wretham Nature Reserve, and walk a short distance from the busy A1075, you will hear waterfowl clanking and splashing on Langmere, songbirds chattering in the gorse, the bleat of sheep and the hiss of the wind whispering through the pine trees. It is difficult to imagine that, during the Second World War, this was a large and bustling military base, with thundering Wellington and Lancaster bombers shattering the peace of the countryside. The Czech Training Unit were also based here, a situation similar to the one depicted in the 2002 film *Dark Blue World*.

Military Airbase
The heath was acquired in 1938 by the Norfolk Naturalists' Trust (now the Norfolk Wildlife Trust), because the sandy scrub contained such a wide variety of plants and animals. Among its treasures are some rare spiders and moths, and unusual butterflies, such as small skipper, brown argus, grayling and Essex. However, nature came second to defence in 1939, and the Trust was obliged to relinquish it to the RAF shortly after. The military remained until 1970, but their concrete airstrips, roads and buildings are slowly being colonised by mosses, lichens and wildflowers such as vipers bugloss, dark mullein and wall pepper, indicating that nature has the upper hand once more.

Breckland Nature Reserve
The heath was the first nature reserve ever established in Breckland. It owes its current form to grazing by sheep and rabbits, which prevent it from becoming scrubland again. The first rabbits were introduced to England just after the Norman Conquest, when their fur and meat were a highly prized commodity. They were farmed in warrens and were rare and expensive – a far cry from their status today! Their sharp teeth prevent the area from being over-colonised by bracken, allowing delicate wildflowers to thrive. These include hair grass, thyme-leaved speedwell, heath bedstraw, harebells and early forget-me-nots.

In the 18th century, a belt of Waterloo pines was planted to shelter the heath from the prevailing winds and to help anchor down the light sandy soil. These days, oaks and birches have joined them, providing a haven for yellowhammers, willow warblers, finches and tree pipets. The old pines have been gnarled and moulded by time and winds, and now form dramatic shapes across the Norfolk skyline.

This unique area is important for all sorts of reasons. It provides a unique habitat for a number of rare or unusual birds, animals, plants and insects. It is also one of the few surviving areas of Breckland that has not been encroached by farms or other human development. For more information on the Brecklands and the conservation programmes that are currently in operation, contact the Norfolk Wildlife Trust.

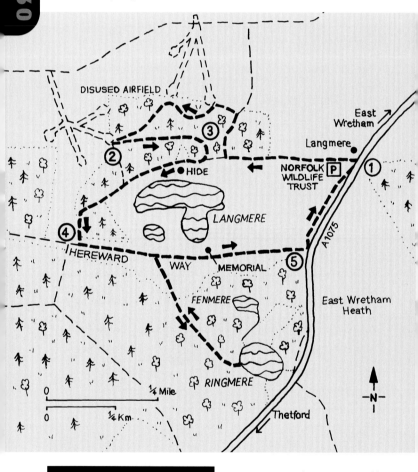

Walk 30 Directions

① From the car park go through the gate and follow the trail marked by green-and-white arrows. This will take you over sandy Breckland heath that is pitted with rabbit warrens, so watch your step. Rabbits can nearly always be seen here. When you reach a kissing gate, follow the green arrow trail that takes you to the right through a pine plantation. You might notice traces of tarmac underfoot, a relic of the airbase.

Walk 30

② At an electric fence with a bench on the other side (!), inspect the area beyond. You may see the crumbling remains of the airfield's concrete and tarmac 'panhandle' dispersal point. Make a sharp left, ignoring the green arrow that will take you on a shorter route, and continue on.

> **WHERE TO EAT AND DRINK** ℹ
> There is nowhere to stop for refreshment on the route, since the entire walk is on a nature reserve. However, the **Dog and Partridge** at nearby East Wretham has good food and a wide range of ales. It has a beer garden at the back, which is a pleasant place to rest after your stroll across the common.

③ Go right at the bend to this path, passing more ruins before you reach a grassy track. Turn right, so that **Langmere** is on your left. A little way down the path is a sign pointing to the bird hide, an excellent place to watch resident waterfowl. However, because the water level in the mere is dependent on the water table (that is, how much water has been extracted artificially, as well as how much it has rained recently), the hide is often

> **WHILE YOU'RE THERE** ℹ
> You can continue walking west along the Drove Road, which is also known as the Hereward Way, to the **Devil's Punchbowl**, a sinister tree-shrouded pool. The town of **Thetford** is also worth a visit. It has one of the tallest castle mounds in the country – about 80ft (24m) – dating from before 1086, along with the remains of a once-powerful Cluniac priory.

flooded, and therefore closed. Continue along the path, following the white arrows. Eventually, you reach another kissing gate.

④ Go through the kissing gate on to old **Drove Road**. This is part of the Hereward Way and is a wide gravel track with fences on either side. The Norfolk Wildlife Trust opens and closes parts of the reserve depending on season and weather conditions, so it is sometimes possible to extend the walk to Ringmere. Hopefully, you will be able to do this, in which case turn right off the Drove Road and, after reaching **Ringmere**, return the same way. Look for notices along the road to see if the path is open. The Drove Road will then take you past the memorial to Sydney Herbert Long, who founded the Norfolk Naturalists' Trust in 1926.

⑤ At the **A1075**, turn left and follow the marker posts back to the car park.

> **WHAT TO LOOK FOR** ℹ
> The **stone curlew** often visits in the summer. You can identify it by its 'coolee' call and, when it is flying, by the white bands on its wings. Look for **crossbills** among the pines, feeding with their sharp beaks among the pine cones. They are not native to the area, but will come if the pine crops fail in Scandinavia.

Lynford's Stag and Arboretum

Walk along the pine-carpeted paths of Thetford Forest, from a metal stag to a mock-Jacobean hall.

•DISTANCE•	4½ miles (7.2km)
•MINIMUM TIME•	2hrs
•ASCENT / GRADIENT•	66ft (20m) ▲ ▲▲ ▲
•LEVEL OF DIFFICULTY•	🚶 🚶 🚶
•PATHS•	Wide grassy trackways and small paths
•LANDSCAPE•	Coniferous and mixed deciduous forest
•SUGGESTED MAP•	aqua3 OS Explorer 229 Thetford Forest in the Brecks
•START / FINISH•	Grid reference: TL 813917
•DOG FRIENDLINESS•	On leads and keep away from children's play areas. No dogs (except guide dogs) in arboretum.
•PARKING•	Lynford Stag picnic site off A134
•PUBLIC TOILETS•	At picnic site

BACKGROUND TO THE WALK

By 1916, with the horrors of the First World War in full swing, the British government realised that it could no longer rely on timber imports to supplement Britain's own wood production and sustain industrial output. The huge demands placed on woodland resources by the onset of trench warfare and the spiralling need for colliery pit props brought the realisation that it would have to establish a group responsible for planting strategic timber reserves, as well as chopping them down again. The solution was the Forestry Commission, established immediately after the war in 1919. It began by buying up large tracts of land that were suitable for growing trees. One of the first areas it obtained was the sandy heathland around the ancient priory town of Thetford, because this was an ideal habitat for many species of fast-growing conifers.

Timber Industry

By 1935, the new Thetford Forest had reached the boundaries on today's maps. It covers an area of approximately 50,000 acres (20,250ha), and is the largest lowland pine forest in the country. Originally, it was dominated by Scots pine, but this was changed to Corsican pine, which allows some 220,000 tons (224,000 tonnes) of timber to be cut every year. This is enough to build a 4ft (1.2m) high plank fence around the entire length of Britain's mainland coast. The amount taken is carefully controlled, so that the timber industry is sustainable – it never takes more than it plants.

Wildlife

The forest is more than just a giant timber-producing yard, however. It is home to numerous rare animals, birds and plants, including the native red squirrel, and people travel from miles around to enjoy the peace of the great forest trackways. Lucky visitors who walk quietly may spot one of the park's four species of resident deer: fallow, roe, red and muntjac.

It is also home to a large number of bats, including the pipistrelle and the barbastelle, that feed on the many insects that inhabit the forest. Because the area is so important to bats, a bat hibernaculum has been built, to give them somewhere to spend the daylight hours.

Unusual Target
Lynford Stag is named for the life-sized metal deer that stands quietly and unobtrusively among the car parks and picnic benches. This was discovered by Forestry Commission workers when they were clearing the area for planting trees, and must have given them quite a surprise. It was made for Sir Richard Sutton, a keen hunter who owned nearby Lynford Hall. He used it for target practice and, if you approach it, you will see the scars of its previous existence.

Lynford Hall
Lynford Hall is a Grade II listed mock-Jacobean mansion standing amid imposing gardens overlooking a series of artificial lakes. The building began in 1857 on the site of an earlier hall dating to the 1720s. The estate was known for the splendid quality of its hunting, and birds and beasts continued to fall until 1924, when the hall was sold to the Forestry Commission. In the late 1940s, trainee foresters began to plant trees in its grounds. These now form the arboretum.

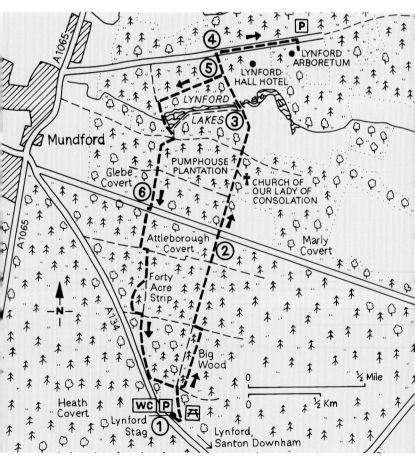

Walk 31

Walk 31 Directions

① Leave the car park and follow the blue marker posts into the trees. Jig slightly to the right and follow the markers heading north. The path then turns left. Take the next wide track to your right, next to a bench, leaving the blue trail to walk along edge of the Christmas tree plantation. Eventually, you reach a paved road.

WHILE YOU'RE THERE ⓘ

Visit the **High Lodge Forest Centre** at Santon Downham, just over the border in Suffolk, if you want more information about the Forestry Commission and what to do in the area. Attractions include cycle hire and the giant Squirrels' Maze. There are also children's activity days, a shop and café, an outdoor theatre and a concert programme. Deeper into Suffolk is **West Stow**, a recreated Saxon village.

---

② Cross the road and continue ahead on what was once part of the driveway leading to Lynford Hall. There is a notice board giving information about the arboretum and its 'lost' Victorian gardens. Go past it to **Pumphouse Plantation** along a gravel path, picking up the next set of blue and green trails. The Church of Our Lady of Consolation is behind the trees to your right. It was designed by Pugin in the 1870s for the owner of the

---

WHERE TO EAT AND DRINK ⓘ

Lynford Hall Hotel is a perfect place to take a break, since it lies at the halfway point. It offers bar meals and morning and afternoon teas and coffees, and is open from 11AM to 11PM. The **Lynford Stag** picnic site has picnic tables and a huge wooden 'play' stag for children. There are ice cream vans here in the summer and on busy weekends.

---

hall who was a Catholic, but the next owner, a Protestant, planted the trees to shield the unattractive building from view. After a few minutes, you reach a stone bridge.

WHAT TO LOOK FOR ⓘ

The **red squirrel**, once a common sight in our woodlands but now sadly depleted in numbers, can be found in the forest. Besides deer, you may also see foxes, hares and badgers. Around the Lynford Lakes and its drains keep an eye out for frogs, toads and newts.

---

③ At the stone bridge across **Lynford Lakes**, a sign gives information about the history of Lynford Hall, now a hotel. Cross the bridge and walk until **Lynford Hall** comes into view. Continue walking past the Hall.

④ At the T-junction, turn right and walk along the road to visit the **arboretum**. When you have finished, retrace your steps along the lane, then turn left so that the Hall is on your left.

⑤ Turn right on to a wide grassy sward called **Sequoia Avenue**. Walk almost to the end of it, then follow the blue markers to the left into the wood. After a few paces you come to the lake. This is a good place to look for frogs and newts. The blue trail bears to the left at the end of the lake, but our walk continues straight ahead on the bridleway. The path jigs left, then right, but keep to the bridleway.

⑥ Cross a paved lane and continue straight on, towards the Christmas trees. Turn left at the end of the track, then almost immediately right, where you will pick up the blue trail markers again. Follow these until you reach the car park.

Blakeney Eye's Magical Marshes

Walk along the sea defences to some of the finest bird reserves in the country.

•DISTANCE•	4½ miles (7.2km)
•MINIMUM TIME•	2hrs
•ASCENT / GRADIENT•	98ft (30m)
•LEVEL OF DIFFICULTY•	
•PATHS•	Footpaths with some paved lanes, can flood in winter
•LANDSCAPE•	Salt marshes, scrubby meadows and farmland
•SUGGESTED MAP•	aqua3 OS Explorer 251 Norfolk Coast Central
•START / FINISH•	Grid reference: TG 028441
•DOG FRIENDLINESS•	Under control as these are important refuges for birds
•PARKING•	Carnser (pay) car park, on seafront opposite Blakeney Guildhall and Manor Hotel
•PUBLIC TOILETS•	Across road from Carnser car park

BACKGROUND TO THE WALK

Blakeney was a prosperous port in medieval times, but went into decline when its sea channels began to silt up. However, although the merchants decried the slow accumulation of salt marsh and sand bars, birds began to flock here in their thousands. By Victorian times it had become such a favoured spot with feathered migrants that it became known as *the* place to go shooting and collecting. Some sportsmen just wanted to kill the many waterfowl, while others were more interested in trophy collecting – looking for species that were rare or little-known. The maxim 'what's hit is history; what's missed is mystery' was very characteristic of the Victorians' attitude to biological science. Many of these hapless birds ended up stuffed in museums or private collections.

Nature Reserve
After many years of bloody slaughter the National Trust arrived in 1912 and purchased the area from Cley Beach to the tip of the sand and shingle peninsula of Blakeney Point. It became one of the first nature reserves to be safeguarded in Britain. Today it is a fabulous place for a walk, regardless of whether you are interested in ornithology. A bright summer day will show you glittering streams, salt-scented grasses waving gently in the breeze and pretty-sailed yachts bobbing in the distance. By contrast, a wet and windy day in winter will reveal the stark beauty of this place, with the distant roar of white-capped waves pounding the beach, rain-drenched vegetation and a menacing low-hung sky filled with scudding clouds. It really doesn't matter what the weather is like at Blakeney, because a walk here is invigorating in any of its moods.

Although these days we regard the Victorians' wholesale slaughter with distaste, they did leave behind them a legacy of valuable information. It was 19th-century trophy hunters who saw the Pallas' warbler and the yellow-breasted bunting in Britain for the first time – and they were seen at Blakeney. A little later, when the Cley Bird Observatory operated here between 1949 and 1963, the first sub-alpine warbler in Norfolk was captured and ringed.

The Victorians' records tell us that a good many red-spotted bluethroats appeared in September and October, and any collector who happened to visit then was almost certain to bag one. In the 1950s the observatory discovered that these were becoming rare at this time of year. Today, bluethroats are regular spring visitors but are seldom seen in the autumn. It is thought that this change over time is related to different weather patterns and indicates how climate change, even on this small scale, can dramatically effect the behaviour of birds.

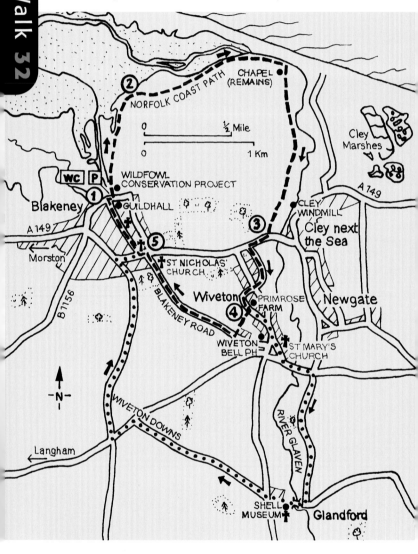

Walk 32 **Directions**

① From the car park head for the wildfowl conservation project, a fenced-off area teeming with ducks, geese and widgeon. A species list has been mounted on one side, so you can see how many you can spot. Take the path marked **Norfolk Coast Path** out towards the marshes. This raised bank is part of

Walk 32

the sea defences, and is managed by the Environment Agency. Eventually, you have salt marshes on both sides.

② At the turning, head east. Carmelite friars once lived around here, although there is little to see of their chapel, the remains of which are located just after you turn by the wooden staithe (landing stage) to head south again. This part of the walk is excellent for spotting kittiwakes and terns in late summer. Also, look for Sabine's gull, manx and sooty shearwaters, godwits, turnstones and curlews. The path leads you past **Cley Windmill,** built in 1810 and which last operated in 1919. It is open to visitors and you can climb to the top to enjoy the view across the marshes. Follow signs for the Norfolk Coast Path until you reach the **A149**.

WHILE YOU'RE THERE ℹ
Langham Glass at nearby Morston, has restored 18th-century workshops, demonstrations and a shop. Morston Marshes are in the care of the National Trust and are an important site for migrating wrynecks, icterine and barred warblers. If you have time, a boat trip out to see the seals is a rewarding experience. These endearing creatures breed and bask on the isolated sandbars to the north.

refreshments before the homeward stretch, turn left and walk a short way to the **Wiveton Bell**. The lane is wide and ahead you will see St Nicholas' Church nestling among trees. This dates from the 13th century, but was extended in the 14th. Its two towers served as navigation beacons for sailors, and the narrower, east one is floodlit at night.

⑤ At the **A149** there are two lanes opposite you. Take the **High Street** fork on the left to walk through the centre of **Blakeney** village. Many cottages are owned by the Blakeney Neighbourhood Housing Society, which rents homes to those locals unable to buy their own. Don't miss the 14th-century Guildhall undercroft at the bottom of Mariner's Hill. Then continue straight ahead into the car park.

WHERE TO EAT AND DRINK ℹ
In Blakeney the Kabin sandwich bar in the car park operates between Easter and October, and sells snacks, tea and coffee. The Blakeney Hotel, Manor Hotel, White Horse and King's Arms all have restaurants and bar food. There are also several shops for picnic supplies. The Moorings Bistro serves tea and coffee as well as meals. On the walk itself you can try the Wiveton Bell.

③ Cross the A149 to the pavement opposite, then turn right. Take the first left after crossing the little creek. Eventually you reach the cobblestone houses of **Wiveton** and a crossroads; go straight ahead.

④ Take the grassy track opposite **Primrose Farm**, and walk along it until you reach a T-junction. This is the **Blakeney Road**, and you turn right along it. However, if you want

WHAT TO LOOK FOR ℹ
Blakeney Point and its marshes comprise one of the best birdwatching areas in Norfolk. What you see depends on the time of year, but in the winter you can expect a huge variety of waterfowl, along with curlews, rock pipets and hen harriers. In early summer, plovers and terns arrive, while high summer and autumn are the best seasons, with the potential for spotting hundreds of different species of birds.

Walk 33

Around Holyhead Mountain

The last stop before Ireland, rugged and rocky Holy Island offers some of the best walking in Anglesey.

•DISTANCE•	4½ miles (7.2km)
•MINIMUM TIME•	2hrs 30min
•ASCENT / GRADIENT•	886ft (270m) ▲▲▲
•LEVEL OF DIFFICULTY•	🚶🚶 🚶🚶 🚶🚶
•PATHS•	Well-maintained paths and tracks
•LANDSCAPE•	Heathland, coastal cliffs and rocky hills
•SUGGESTED MAP•	aqua3 OS Explorer 262 Anglesey West
•START / FINISH•	Grid reference: SH 210818
•DOG FRIENDLINESS•	Dogs should be on leads at all times
•PARKING•	RSPB car park
•PUBLIC TOILETS•	Just up road from car park

BACKGROUND TO THE WALK

Anglesey's flat – everybody knows that from geography lessons at school – and when you motor along the fast and busy A5 to Holyhead the flat fields flashing by the car window confirm the fact. It comes as a surprise then, that when you leave the main road and pass Trearddur Bay, the green fields turn to rugged heathland that rises to a rocky hillside. The locals and the mapmakers call it Holyhead Mountain, and it matters little that it rises to a mere 722ft (220m) above the waves, because this mountain rises steep and craggy and looks out across those waves to Ireland.

Breeding Grounds
The path from the car park heads straight for a white castellated building known as Ellin's Tower. This former summerhouse is now an RSPB seabird centre. The surrounding area is a breeding ground for puffins, guillemots, razorbills and the rare mountain chough (What to Look For): a closed-circuit video camera shows live pictures of these birds. Outside you can look across to the little island of South Stack, with its lighthouse perched on high cliffs.

Although the cliff scenery is stunning, a rather nasty concrete shelter and the radar dishes of a BT station spoil the early scenes, but they're soon left behind as you make your way towards that rocky 'mountain'.

Across the Heath
In this area the footpath traverses splendid maritime heath dominated by heather, bell heather and stunted western gorse. The rare spotted rock rose also grows here, it looks a little like the common rock rose but has red spots on its yellow petals.

The footpath eventually climbs over the shoulder of a ridge connecting the summit and North Stack. You'll see a direct path heading for the summit when you reach this ridge. It's a bit of a scramble in places, but worth doing if you're fit and there are no young children in your party. Otherwise, the best route for the more sedate rambler is to head along the ridge towards North Stack.

North Stack

After a short climb there's a big drop down a zig-zag path to reach a rocky knoll with a splendid view down to North Stack, another tiny island. On the mainland, adjacent, there's a Fog Signal Station which warns shipping away from the more treacherous waters.

The Boats to Ireland

Now the walk cuts across more heath along the north east side of Holyhead Mountain. From here you'll be looking over Holyhead town and its huge harbour. Once a small fishing village, Holyhead came to prominence after the Act of Union 1821, when its convenient position for travel to Ireland made it the ideal choice for shipping routes. The big ferries and 'cats' will be a feature of this last leg, for you'll surely see at least one glide out of the bay.

Walk 33 Directions

① Take the path signed for the RSPB centre, past **Ellin's Tower**, a small castellated building, then climb along the path back to the road which should be followed to its end.

② If you're not visiting the South Stack Lighthouse, climb right on a path passing a concrete shelter. The path detours right to round the BT aerials and dishes. At a crossroads go left, heading back to the coast, then take the left fork. Ignore the next left, a dead end path. The footpath required works its way over the north shoulder of **Holyhead Mountain**.

WHILE YOU'RE THERE ℹ️

It's worth seeing the **South Stack Lighthouse Visitor Centre** while you're here. You get there by descending 160 steps down to a suspension bridge to the island. You can tour the exhibition area and see the engine room before climbing to the top of the lighthouse tower. Open Easter to September.

---

③ Ignore paths to the summit, but keep left on a good path heading north towards **North Stack**.

④ After passing through a grassy walled enclosure the path descends in zig-zags down some steep slopes before coming to a rocky platform, where the **Fog Signal Station** and the island of North Stack come into full view. Retrace your steps back up the zig-zags and towards Holyhead Mountain.

WHERE TO EAT AND DRINK ℹ️

There is a basic **café** near the RSPB centre. The **Trearddur Bay Hotel** is a large hotel overlooking the sea. Here the Inn at the Bay is more informal than the hotel restaurant and makes use of a conservatory.

---

⑤ With the summit path in sight, take a narrow path heading sharp left across the heath. This joins another narrow path contouring round the east side of the mountain. Turn right along it, later ignoring another summit path coming in from the left. Beyond the mountain, take a

---

WHAT TO LOOK FOR ℹ️

Holy Island is one of the few places in the United Kingdom where **choughs** live and breed. Part of the crow family, the chough is a large black bird with a red bill. Its aerobatics are rather like those of its cousin, the raven, and it nests in crevices in the sea cliffs, where it quarrels regularly with the sea birds.

---

right fork as the path comes to a wall. Follow the path downhill towards rough pastureland.

⑥ Go down a grassy walled track before turning right along another, similar one. This soon becomes a rough path traversing more heathland, now to the south of Holyhead Mountain.

⑦ Near to a quarry with a lake, take the path veering right alongside the rocks of the Holyhead Mountain. The BT aerials and dishes can be seen again on the horizon by now. Follow paths towards them then, at a crossroads, turn left and left again, along a concrete footpath leading back to the road.

⑧ Turn left along the road to the car park.

Birds, Beasts and Butterflies at Tittesworth

Reservoir biodiversity provides drinking water for the Potteries and a valuable habitat for lots of wildlife.

•DISTANCE•	4¼ miles (6.8km)
•MINIMUM TIME•	3hrs
•ASCENT / GRADIENT•	131ft (40m) ▲ ▲ ▲
•LEVEL OF DIFFICULTY•	🚶 🚶 🚶
•PATHS•	Good well-made footpaths, forest tracks and roads
•LANDSCAPE•	Reservoir and woodland
•SUGGESTED MAP•	aqua3 OS Explorer OL24 White Peak
•START / FINISH•	Grid reference: SK 999603
•DOG FRIENDLINESS•	Suitable for dogs
•PARKING•	Near Middle Hulme Farm
•PUBLIC TOILETS•	At reservoir visitor centre

BACKGROUND TO THE WALK

Tittesworth Reservoir and dam were built in 1858 to collect water from the River Churnet and provide a reliable water supply to Leek's thriving textile and cloth dying industry. By 1963 work to increase its size had been completed and local farmland was flooded to create a reservoir capable of supplying drinking water to Stoke-on-Trent and surrounding areas. With a capacity of 6½ billion gallons (29½ billion litres), when full it can supply 10 million gallons (45 million litres) of water every day.

Habitat for Wildlife

The land around the reservoir provides a habitat for a wide variety of wildlife and many creatures can be seen in the course of this walk. Look out for brown hares in the fields near the car park. You can tell them from rabbits by their very long legs, black-tipped ears and a triangular black and light brown tail.

Otters were once hunted almost to extinction by dogs and although the sport is now illegal their numbers remain low. They are nocturnal creatures and not often seen, but look out for their droppings by the water's edge and the tell-tale prints of their webbed feet and wavy line tail prints in the sand and soft mud. Look also for holes in the banks along the River Churnet, where it enters the reservoir. Although he's a difficult little creature to spot, a hole may just be the entrance to a vole burrow and home to a water vole like Ratty from *The Wind in the Willows*.

Bats and Birds

Europe's smallest bat, the pipistrelle, suffered a severe decline in numbers in the last decades of the 20th century due to loss of hunting habitats like hedges, ponds and grassland. Pond restoration near Churnet Bay is encouraging their return and they can best be seen here near dusk, flying at an incredible speed, twisting and turning as they dive to gobble caddisflies, moths and gnats.

Bird life around the reservoir is also abundant and there are two bird hides from which visitors can observe in comfort. Look out particularly for skylarks, small birds with a high-pitched continuous warble, that nest in the meadows around Tittesworth. The song thrush, another bird that has been in decline, also finds a home here, as does the linnet. Look especially for the male of the species in spring and summer when it has a bright blood-red breast and forehead. You'll find them in the trees and bushes near the visitor centre and at the hide near the conservation pool.

At various times of the year you might spot barnacle geese, great crested grebe, pied flycatchers, spectacular kingfishers, cormorants and even a rare osprey that has visited here several times in recent years.

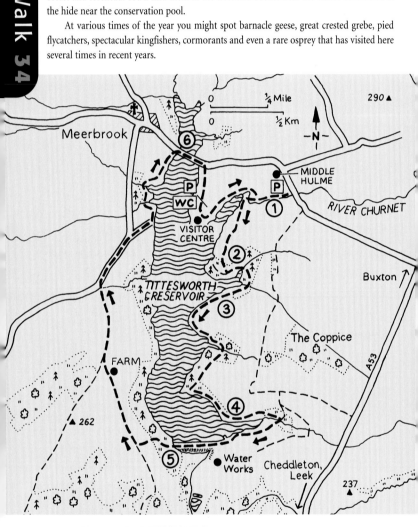

Walk 34 Directions

① Go through a gate on to a footpath and turn right. Cross the first bridge, turn left then cross a second bridge and follow the Long Trail/Short Trail direction signs along a well-surfaced path. At a junction beside a picnic table turn left on to a forest trail.

② Follow the waymarked **Long Trail** through the wood crossing a bridge and some duckboarding then turn left at a T-junction again

> ### WHILE YOU'RE THERE ⓘ
> A visit to the **Churnet Valley Railway** will invoke memories of steam travel on a rural railway of the mid-20th century. Starting from the Victorian station at Cheddleton, it meanders along beside the River Churnet and the Cauldon Canal. There are several stops including the picturesque hamlet of Consall with some fine local walks and the Black Lion public house.

following the Long Trail. Follow the path as it leaves the wood and on to a grassy area where it is less well defined but still visible.

③ Continue along the bank of the reservoir then re-enter woodland, cross some duckboards and continue once more on a well-defined footpath. Cross a bridge by a picnic table, ascend some steps and continue along duckboards. Skirt the edge of a wood, keeping the fence on your left, then go downhill through a wood and along the reservoir bank.

> ### WHAT TO LOOK FOR ⓘ
> Towards the end of the walk look out for **Butterfly Beach** an experimental area designed to encourage breeding butterflies. This 'luxury hotel' for these delightful insects has a sandy beach for a spot of sunbathing on a warm summer day and thistles, nettles and a host of wild flowers to provide egg laying sites and food.

④ Go through some more woodland, cross a bridge, walk up some steps then leave the wood and continue on a gravel path. Cross a stile then follow the path downhill towards the dam. Go over a stile and cross the dam head. Cross a stile at the far end, go uphill on a series of steps and turn right on to a footpath.

⑤ Cross a stile and turn right at a T-junction on to a metalled lane. Continue on this through a farm, following the signs for Meerbrook, straight ahead. At the road junction cross a stile and turn right at the **Long Trail** sign. Turn right again following the road to **Tittesworth Reservoir**. When this turns to the right, bear left on a footpath beside the reservoir.

⑥ Cross another stile on to the road then turn right into the public entrance to the reservoir. Turn left at the entrance to the visitor centre, cross the car park then go left at the Nature Trail sign. Continue across the grass then turn right on to a concrete path. Follow this to the first bridge then turn left to return to the car park.

> ### WHERE TO EAT AND DRINK ⓘ
> Stop at the **Tittesworth Visitor Centre** which is on the walk. This light and airy restaurant has great views over the water and a good selection of food options ranging from a full breakfast through tasty soups and rolls to afternoon teas with delicious scones and pastries.

Walk 35

Squirrels and Sand at Formby Point

The effort is minimal and the rewards are great on this exhilarating walk through an area of great significance for wildlife.

•DISTANCE•	3½ miles (5.7km)
•MINIMUM TIME•	1hr 30min
•ASCENT / GRADIENT•	50ft (15m)
•LEVEL OF DIFFICULTY•	
•PATHS•	Well-worn paths through woods and salt marsh, plus long stretch of sand
•LANDSCAPE•	Pine forest, sand dunes and a vast sweep of beach
•SUGGESTED MAP•	aqua3 OS Explorer 285 Southport & Chorley
•START / FINISH•	Grid reference: SD 278082
•DOG FRIENDLINESS•	On leads in nature reserve but can run free on beach
•PARKING•	Either side of access road just beyond kiosk
•PUBLIC TOILETS•	At start

BACKGROUND TO THE WALK

It has to be said that most of the Cheshire and Lancashire coast is fairly urbanised. And as you approach through the town of Formby there's little to suggest that here will be any different. It seems to be somewhere to retire to, or perhaps to commute to Liverpool. This makes Formby Point all the more remarkable.

Tall, shady pine woods form your first impression. They may appear ancient but were actually planted less than 100 years ago, to help stabilise the sand dunes. No one at the time could have suspected that they would become such an important haven for red squirrels.

The dark peaty soils that occur inland of the dunes produce a variety of crops, but a particular local specialty is asparagus. You may still see this growing in the fields that border the reserve early in the walk. On the way out towards the shore you pass a lake, natural in origin, where swans, ducks, coots and moorhens breed.

Miles of Dunes

The sand dunes at Formby form the largest dune system in England. The line of dunes immediately behind the beach is partly stabilised by the rough-edged marram grass, but high tides and high winds can still change their shape in a matter of hours. The feet of visitors also erode the fragile dunes.

The beach itself is littered with patches of shell debris. Under the sand there are many invertebrates which attract wading birds. One of the easiest to recognise is the oystercatcher, black and white apart from its bright orange eyes, beak and legs. Many other waders and gulls may also be sighted.

As you walk along below the dunes, you will see some darker layers exposed by erosion of the sand. These sediments were formed around 4,000 years ago, when the shape of the coast was somewhat different. In places they have been found to preserve the tracks of animals and birds, so that we know, for instance, that oystercatchers were plentiful then too.

Human footprints have also been found. These suggest that people hunted and fished here, but the most evocative report is of a medley of small prints suggesting children at play.

A Haven for Wildlife

From the end of the beach you wind through the sand hills again, past pools where natterjack toads – one of Britain's rarest animals – breed. You'll need to be lucky indeed to see one. Two other rarities that are also found here are great crested newts, around the pools, and sand lizards, in the drier areas.

Finally the walk returns through woods again to the start. Apart from squirrels you may see treecreepers, small brown birds that – as their name suggests – crawl all over the bark of the trees looking for insects.

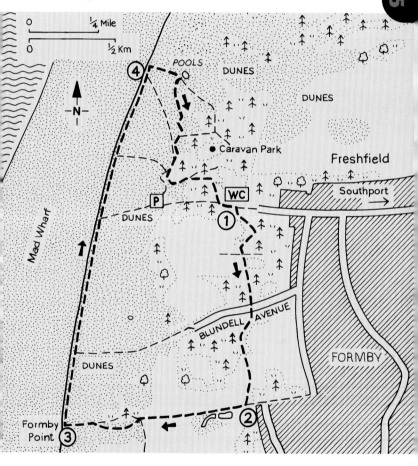

Walk 35 **Directions**

① Start just left of the large notice board. Follow the 'Squirrel Walk', with its wooden fencing, to the left and then round to the right. Keep

straight on at a crossroads, where there's a sign for Blundell Avenue. There are many subsidiary paths but the main line runs virtually straight ahead to **Blundell Avenue**. Cross the avenue to a fainter path almost opposite, with a 'No Cycling'

Walk 35

sign and traces of bricks in its surface. Follow this, skirting around the edge of a field (brick traces are still a useful guide). Go up a slight rise then across more open sand hills to a line of pines on a rise ahead. Skirt left round a hollow and you'll see some houses ahead.

② Just before reaching the houses turn right on a straight track. This swings left slightly then forks. Go right, down steps, then straight on down the side of a reed-fringed pool. Beyond this keep fairly straight on, towards the sand hills. When you reach them swing left then right, picking up a boardwalk, to skirt the highest dunes and so out to the beach.

> **WHILE YOU'RE THERE** ℹ
> One way to get to **Southport** would be simply to keep walking along the sands. It's a resort that retains much of the genteel flavour of its Victorian heyday. Amenities are largely as you'd expect, with a boating lake and amusement park, a small zoo and an aviary in Hesketh Park. At low tide the sea can be miles away and instead of windsurfers you'll probably see land yachts.

③ Turn right along the open and virtually level sand. The firmest walking surface is usually some way out from the base of the dunes. Walk parallel to these (heading north) for over 1¼ miles (2km). The shoreline curves very gently to the

> **WHERE TO EAT AND DRINK** ℹ
> The excellent **Freshfield Hotel** (turn left at the junction about 400yds (366m) east of the level crossing) only serves its good-value food on weekday lunchtimes. This could be a good reason to time your visit accordingly, especially if you're a lover of real ale. At other times, or if you've children in tow, try the **Grapes**, at the other end of Massams Lane.

right but there are few distinctive landmarks apart from signs to various approach paths. It would be all too easy to just keep on going, so watch for a sign for the **Gipsy Wood Path**.

④ A distinct track winds through sand hills then swings more decisively to the right near some pools, where there's a sign board about natterjack toads. Follow the track back into woods and, at a junction, go right. The track curves round between woods and sand hills then joins a wider track by a Sefton Coastal Footpath sign. Go through a patch of willows then bear left to a line of pines on a rise. From these drop down to a broad path with a gravelly surface and follow it left into woods again. Stick to the main path, with timber edgings and white-topped posts, bear right by a large 'xylophone', and it leads quickly back to the start.

> **WHAT TO LOOK FOR** ℹ
> You'll probably not need to walk too far or look too hard before encountering the **red squirrel** colony. Once familiar throughout England, they have largely been supplanted by grey squirrels, originally from North America, but the wide treeless expanses inland from Formby have helped keep them away here. A much greater rarity, which you'll be lucky to see, is the **natterjack toad**.

Lancashire's 'Fens' and Martin Mere

An easy walk on the West Lancashire Plain, under wide skies, around a great bird centre.

•DISTANCE•	5 miles (8km)
•MINIMUM TIME•	2hrs
•ASCENT / GRADIENT•	50ft (15m)
•LEVEL OF DIFFICULTY•	
•PATHS•	Canal tow paths, lanes, farm tracks and field paths, 2 stiles
•LANDSCAPE•	Flat and open farmland with glimpses of wilder wetland
•SUGGESTED MAP•	aqua3 OS Explorer 285 Southport & Chorley
•START / FINISH•	Grid reference: SD 423126
•DOG FRIENDLINESS•	On leads across farmland but can be let off on tow path
•PARKING•	Several small lay-bys near mid-point of Gorst Lane
•PUBLIC TOILETS•	Nothing near by, unless using Martin Mere Visitor Centre

BACKGROUND TO THE WALK

The levels of south west Lancashire seem to provide easy travelling: there are miles of canal with no locks and roads and railways with scarcely an incline – and there's easy walking too. However, for most of history these lowlands were an obstacle. Ancient roads and trackways follow the high ground because, until well into the 18th century, this gave easier travelling.

The Lancashire Mosslands

The Industrial Revolution was closely paralleled by, and to some extent depended on, an agricultural revolution. In many cases the same engineers who built the great canals were also responsible for great drainage schemes. The flat peat Lancashire mosslands were largely transformed into farmland. They fed the growing towns elsewhere in the county with green vegetables, carrots and, above all, potatoes.

Only a few pockets of mossland survive in anything like their original state. Leighton Moss is one and the Martin Mere reserve, once a lake, possibly the largest in Lancashire, is another. It's no accident that both are now centres of huge importance for wildlife and especially for birds.

Wildfowl Reserve

Martin Mere is one of nine centres in the UK run by the Wildfowl and Wetlands Trust, founded by Sir Peter Scott. The reserve itself plays host to a wide variety of resident and migrant birds. Breeding species range from reed and sedge warblers and reed buntings to the spectacular marsh harrier. However, it's the massive flocks of winter visitors that create the most spectacular displays.

The reserve is merely a kind of nucleus and great numbers of geese and swans gather on the fields around, often partly flooded in the winter months. A particular feature is the large number of pink-footed geese – but don't assume that geese with pink feet are necessarily pink-footed geese! They might be greylags – but these are larger and heavier, with longer bills, and may be seen all year round.

Please note that the Wildfowl and Wetlands Trust asks walkers to avoid the paths nearest to the reserve at certain times – specifically from 1 October to 1 April. The reason is that if disturbed the birds may settle further away, on land owned by less sympathetic farmers, and risk being shot. You can't altogether blame the farmers as the birds can virtually strip fields of their growing crops. This request should be heeded and an alternative route is given. You may also want to bear in mind that the ground can be wet at this time of year and you might find the walk more comfortable in wellies.

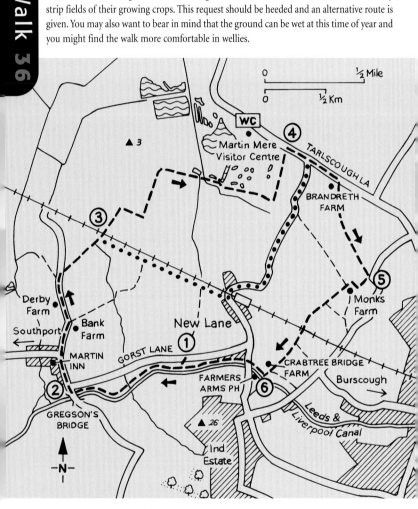

Walk 36 Directions

① Near the mid-point of **Gorst Lane** there's a small timber yard. Follow a short track up through this to meet the canal by a small swing bridge. Go right along the tow path and follow it for about ¾ mile (1.2km) to **Gregson's Bridge**. Go under the bridge then up to a lane.

② Join a wider road (**Martin Lane**) and follow it away from the canal for about 350yds (320m). At a bend, by the **Martin Inn**, bear right down a narrow lane. Follow this for about 700yds (640m), past the

The largest birds you'll see and, certainly in terms of weight, the largest wild birds in Britain, are **swans**. There are three species. Mute swans are the most widespread, with curved necks and orange bills. Whooper and Bewick's swans both have yellow bills, but Bewick's are smaller, with thicker necks – altogether more goose-like. Only mute swans breed regularly in Britain.

farm, to a very open section. Opposite some glasshouses there's a footpath sign on the right. Follow the track to the railway line.

③ Cross the line and continue down the track until you come to a green shed. Go right, alongside a drainage ditch, until another ditch appears ahead. Go left alongside this. Continue to a stile by a gate then swing right alongside a reed-lined channel. Follow this over two bridges, the second bridge being close to the corner of the **Martin Mere Reserve**. Continue down a green track, following the edge of the reserve, out to a road (**Tarlscough Lane**).

④ Turn right and follow the road for 500yds (457m). Immediately past **Brandreth Farm** there's a footpath sign. Go down the side of a large shed, go right then left round a pool and on down an obvious track.

⑤ When you reach the end of the track, just before a lane, turn right on a concrete track. Turn right before a house and follow the fence round to the left. Keep almost straight on, past another signpost, and follow a well-trodden footpath through crops towards a couple of trees. These act as direction posts down the field edges to the railway

line. Cross and keep straight on, following the slightly raised line of old field boundaries, then join a track to and through **Crabtree Bridge Farm**.

⑥ Swing right on the tow path. It's about 200yds (183m) to the swing bridge by the **Farmers Arms** and another 500yds (457m) to the smaller one above the timber yard. Drop back down through this to **Gorst Lane**.

WHERE TO EAT AND DRINK ℹ
Two pubs in 5 miles (8km) sounds like a recipe for a jolly walk. Actually the **Farmers Arms** is 50yds (46m) off the direct route of the walk, over the swing bridge. It has both pub and restaurant food including 'create your own pizzas'. Outside tables are a bit close to the car park but have a view of the canal. There's also the **Pinkfoot Pantry** at the Martin Mere Reserve.

Important Note
During the main bird migration season (1 October to 1 April) you're requested to avoid the path immediately alongside the reserve. When this applies, an alternative route is as follows: turn right just before the first railway crossing (Point ③). Walk alongside the line to New Lane Station. Turn left up Marsh Moss Lane to the junction with Tarlscough Lane and rejoin the main route.

WHILE YOU'RE THERE ℹ
Having skirted the **Martin Mere Reserve**, take a look at its 350 acres (142ha). The meres, lined with reeds and trees, are a lot closer to the 'natural' landscape of the area than the bare surrounding farmland. The hides give closer views of many birds – and by paying the admission charge you're supporting the work of the Wildfowl and Wetlands Trust.

Moors at the Centre

A tough walk that gives a chance to taste the freedom of the high moors.

•DISTANCE•	9¼ miles (14.9km)
•MINIMUM TIME•	3hrs 30min
•ASCENT / GRADIENT•	1,247ft (380m) ▲▲▲
•LEVEL OF DIFFICULTY•	🚶 🚶 🚶
•PATHS•	Field paths, rougher moorland paths, surfaced road, 9 stiles
•LANDSCAPE•	Rough pasture, exposed moorland, sheltered valley
•SUGGESTED MAP•	aqua3 OS Explorer OL41 Forest of Bowland & Ribblesdale
•START / FINISH•	Grid reference: SD 660501
•DOG FRIENDLINESS•	Grazing land, keep dogs on leads
•PARKING•	Public car park at Dunsop Bridge
•PUBLIC TOILETS•	At car park

BACKGROUND TO THE WALK

There aren't many places where a phone box is a tourist attraction, but the one at Dunsop Bridge is deemed to stand at the centre point of Great Britain. This apart, Dunsop Bridge lacks amusements for less energetic visitors, but it lacks nothing for magnificent surroundings and is the starting point for many great walks. This route uses something which is quite a rarity in Bowland, a public footpath crossing the tops.

To the Tops

To reach it you cross a stretch of upland pasture. This gives straightforward walking, rarely steep, except where it dips into Oxenhurst Clough. The clough frames a view of the small conical hill called Knot or Sugar Loaf, which began as a coral reef around 250 million years ago. The ascent to the plateau is by a well-defined ridge, giving wider views than from the level top. The prospect takes in the Hodder Valley, Stocks Reservoir and Gisburn Forest, the broader sweep of Ribblesdale and the Yorkshire hills.

Heather Moors

The heather moors of Bowland have traditionally been managed principally for grouse shooting. In recent years, for reasons that are not fully understood, grouse numbers have declined substantially. This has affected the livelihood of many local people and has had a knock-on effect on other species. Hen harriers, for instance, prey in part on grouse chicks.

The Birds of Bowland Project

In the past walkers, conservationists and shooting interests have sometimes viewed each other suspiciously. Gamekeepers have been accused of poisoning birds of prey. Today, however, there is a new spirit of co-operation. The Birds of Bowland Project involves the RSPB, United Utilities (a major landowner) and receives funding from the Heritage Lottery Fund and Ribble Valley District Council. The aim is to encourage sympathetic management of the distinctive habitat and to protect the bird populations. One result should be to encourage more visitors to the area, something which should be further helped by the much wider access to open country that has recently been achieved.

The moorland crossing may seem all too brief before the descent into Whitendale. Here there are reminders that Bowland is a significant water catchment. Although there's only one large reservoir (Stocks), water is extracted from many of the streams and rivers. The track which you join near Whitendale Farm is actually the line of a water pipe: BCWW stands for Blackburn Corporation Water Works. The main waterworks intake is a little further down the valley and from there you follow the access road most of the way back to Dunsop Bridge.

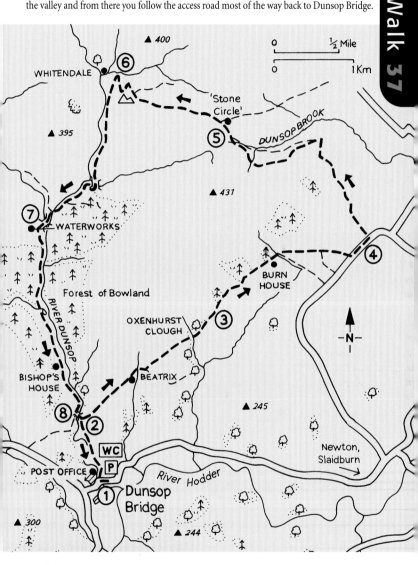

Walk 37 Directions

① From the public car park in Dunsop Bridge, go up a surfaced track, just to the left of the **post office** and tea room, for about 800yds (732m). When you reach the end of the track, by some houses, follow a public footpath for another 100yds (91m) then go right, up a steep bank.

Walk 37

② Cross the large field, bearing slightly left to meet power lines. Continue to a stile just before **Beatrix farm**. Follow the track round the farm until it swings back right again. Go left, through the second of two gates. Climb the slope right of a small stream, over a stile, then follow a wire fence across the hillside. Drop into **Oxenhurst Clough** then climb out through a plantation, rejoining the fence as the gradient eases. Keep straight on to join another track.

WHAT TO LOOK FOR ⓘ

The **hen harrier** is the symbol of the Forest of Bowland. Numbers have declined, but the area remains their best breeding ground in England. Males have greyish backs, females are brown, but both sexes have a white patch at the base of the tail, which helps distinguish them from the similarly-sized buzzard.

---

③ Follow the track for ¾ mile (1.2km) to **Burn House**, where it swings right. Bear away left, across an open field, towards the middle of a young plantation. Follow the path through it, bearing right to a stile. Aim just right of another young plantation in a dip, then across a field towards some houses (**Laythams**). Go left on the lane for 300yds (274m).

④ Turn left up a metalled track. Clearly marked gates guide you round a house. About 50yds (46m) above this, drop to the stream and continue up to its left. From the top of the enclosure a path rises to the right alongside an obvious groove, then swings back left. Climb steadily up a ridge and then swing rightwards above the upper reaches of **Dunsop Brook**. Cross a broad plateau, roughly parallel to an old wall, to a circular patch of stones.

WHERE TO EAT AND DRINK ⓘ

Puddleducks' Tearoom at Dunsop Bridge has teas, cakes and scones but for more substantial fare head east for 2 miles (3.3km) to Newton. The 18th-century **Parkers Arms** has a large beer garden with great views across the Hodder Valley to Easington Fell. The food, served from 12 noon until 9PM, has won awards, and the beer lives up to it.

---

⑤ Turn left and cross the wall at a stile. The path ahead is rough but always clear. After a slight rise it starts to descend, gently at first but gradually getting steeper. As the ground really steepens, descend in big zig-zags, with a gate halfway down. Just above the farm at **Whitendale** go left.

⑥ Follow a conspicuously level track for ¾ mile (1.2km) until it swings round a little side valley, over a couple of footbridges. Go over a stile and wind down to a track by the river. Follow this down to a bridge by some **waterworks**.

⑦ Cross the bridge, join the road and follow it steadily down the valley for 1½ miles (2.4km), past **Bishop's House**.

⑧ Just after a cattle grid, cross the river on a substantial footbridge. Just beyond this you rejoin the outward route.

WHILE YOU'RE THERE ⓘ

Wander through the Hodder Valley to **Slaidburn**, a tidy village of old stone houses. The church, with its box pews and sanctuary pole, is a principal feature. The old grammar school is now a junior school, while the pub, the Hark to Bounty, contained a courtroom, still in use until 1937. Beyond Slaidburn are Stocks Reservoir and Gisburn Forest, offering many walks and cycle routes.

Gisburn Forest – a Walk in the Woods

Wooded valleys and heathland – accompanied by the sounds of woodland birds and waterfowl.

•DISTANCE•	3 miles (4.8km)
•MINIMUM TIME•	1hr 30min
•ASCENT / GRADIENT•	285ft (87m) ▲▲▲
•LEVEL OF DIFFICULTY•	🚶 🚶🚶 🚶🚶
•PATHS•	Forest tracks and footpaths
•LANDSCAPE•	Wooded valleys, forest, beckside heathland
•SUGGESTED MAP•	aqua3 OS Explorer OL41 Forest of Bowland & Ribblesdale
•START / FINISH•	Grid reference: SD 732565
•DOG FRIENDLINESS•	Fine for dogs under reasonable control
•PARKING•	Stocks Reservoir car park, Gisburn Forest (free of charge)
•PUBLIC TOILETS•	None on route

BACKGROUND TO THE WALK

Perfectly placed between the Yorkshire Dales and the Forest of Bowland, Gisburn Forest in the Upper Hodder Valley is the setting for this short, circular stroll. Don't be put off because it's in a forest – it certainly isn't a dire trek through the darkness of a dense conifer plantation. You will walk along open, naturally wooded valleys, beside a tumbling beck and over heathland. You will have views over the reservoir and up to the fells, and you will hear the woodland birdsong and the call of the wildfowl on the water. If you're lucky, you may spot a deer, footprints in the sandy earth confirm their presence.

Stocks Reservoir

The two defining aspects of this walk are the open waters of Stocks Reservoir and the woodlands of Gisburn Forest. The reservoir was built in the 1930s to provide drinking water for the towns of central Lancashire. The village of Stocks was submerged in the process along with many ancient farmsteads. The date stone from one of these can now be seen over the doorway of the post office in Tosside. It was formed by damming the River Hodder and can hold 2.6 billion gallons (12 billion litres) of water when it is at full capacity.

Attractively placed on the edge of the forest, the reservoir is now an important site for wildfowl and 30 different species visit during the average winter period. Amongst the less-commonly sighted of these are red-throated divers, whooper swans, gadwalls and great crested grebes. Amongst the different birds of prey who frequent the area, ospreys and peregrine falcons have been spotted, as well as a rare passing marsh harrier. A birdwatching hide is provided for budding ornithologists, and a pleasant permissive footpath has been constructed around the shoreline.

The Forestry Commission's extensive woodland known as Gisburn Forest was developed at the same time as the reservoir and was opened by HRH Prince George in July 1932. It covers 3,000 acres (1,214ha), making it the largest single forested area in

Lancashire. There are several waymarked trails to be enjoyed, and a cycle network has been developed extending to over 10 miles (16km). Although the majority of the plantations are of the monotonous coniferous variety and are managed principally as a commercial crop, more and more broadleaf trees are being planted to improve the visual aspect and to increase the diversity of wildlife. The forest and the reservoir are now managed in tandem, with inputs from United Utilities, the Forestry Commission and local parishes, to develop a sustainable economic base for this beautiful landscape.

Walk 38 **Directions**

① Leave **Stocks Reservoir car park** in a south easterly direction (straight ahead from the right of the two vehicular entrances). Walk for approximately ¼ mile (400m) then turn left on a forest track marked with a wooden public footpath sign; a red marker post soon confirms your route. There are

good views right, through the trees to the reservoir and causeway with the fells in the background. Keep on the track as it takes you beside open wooded valleys and through natural woodland with a river down on your right.

② Follow the red marker post, set a little off to the right, as it leads you down on to a footpath. The footpath continues with a stream

Walk 38

WHERE TO EAT AND DRINK ⓘ

Nothing is available within the forest itself, so it might be an idea to pack a picnic. Slaidburn, 4½ miles (7.2km) south, has some cafés and the famous 13th-century **Hark to Bounty Inn** which serves good bar meals. **Dunsop Bridge** is a pretty little café stop with the river flowing besides the village green spilling out its flock of mallards on to the grass – especially when the visitors are lunching.

---

wall. Walk straight through **Swinshaw Top** car park to the road and go straight over to take a narrow footpath through the woods by another red marker post. The path opens on to a broadish green swathe but is soon closed in again; however lovely elevated views over the reservoir, left, and the fells ahead make the start of your descent pleasurable.

on your left, across a low footbridge to the opposite bank. Soon the tumbling peaty **Bottoms Beck** is on your right with patches of reeds to the left, until a raised embankment leads to higher ground as you pass the farmland of **Hesbert Hall** to the right.

③ Follow the next red marker post as it directs you left to leave the beck, and walk just a few paces to cross straight over a forest track. Follow the path as it takes you gently uphill over boardwalks and heathland, through upright gateposts by an old broken down

---

WHILE YOU'RE THERE ⓘ

The **Forest of Bowland** is a designated Area of Outstanding Natural Beauty (AONB) occupying the north eastern corner of Lancashire. It is a landscape of barren gritstone fells, moorland and steep sided valleys, with 3,260 acres (1,320ha) of open country available to walkers. The village of Dunsop Bridge in the Trough of Bowland claims to be the official centre of the country – a telephone box adjacent to the village green marks the precise spot.

---

④ Meet a forest track at a bend, proceed straight ahead (slightly right) and follow the track for 200yds (183m) until red posts turn you right, down a footpath with a stream on the right. At a T-junction of footpaths, turn left across open heathland on a clear path back to the car park.

WHAT TO LOOK FOR ⓘ

It's more a case of what to listen for! The **birdsong** throughout the walk, from tiny wrens darting into the bushes in front, to the cry of the curlew skyward is symphonic. Add to that the call of the wildfowl on the reservoir, never far away, and the orchestration is complete.

Walk 39

Golden Acre and Breary Marsh

A walk of great variety in the rolling countryside to the north of Leeds.

•DISTANCE•	5 miles (8km)
•MINIMUM TIME•	2hrs 30min
•ASCENT / GRADIENT•	100ft (30m)
•LEVEL OF DIFFICULTY•	
•PATHS•	Good paths, tracks and quiet roads, 21 stiles
•LANDSCAPE•	Parkland, woods and arable country
•SUGGESTED MAP•	aqua3 OS Explorer 297 Lower Wharfedale
•START / FINISH•	Grid reference: SE 266418
•DOG FRIENDLINESS•	On lead when in park, due to wildfowl
•PARKING•	Golden Acre Park car park, across road from park itself, on A660 just south of Bramhope
•PUBLIC TOILETS•	Golden Acre Park, at start of walk

BACKGROUND TO THE WALK

Leeds is fortunate to have so many green spaces. Some, like Roundhay Park, are long established; others, like the Kirkstall Valley nature reserve, have been created from post-industrial wasteland. But none have had a more chequered history than Golden Acre Park, 6 miles (9.7km) north of the city on the main A660.

Amusement Park

The park originally opened in 1932 as an amusement park. The attractions included a miniature railway, nearly 2 miles (3.2km) in length, complete with dining car. The lake was the centre of much activity, with motor launches, dinghies for hire and races by the Yorkshire Hydroplane Racing Squadron. An open-air lido known, somewhat exotically, as the Blue Lagoon, offered unheated swimming and the prospect of goose-pimples. The Winter Gardens Dance Hall boasted that it had 'the largest dance floor in Yorkshire'.

Though visitors initially flocked to Golden Acre Park, the novelty soon wore off. By the end of the 1938 season the amusement park had closed down and was sold to Leeds City Council. The site was subsequently transformed into botanical gardens – a process that's continued ever since. The hillside overlooking the lake has been lovingly planted with trees and unusual plants, including rock gardens and fine displays of rhododendrons.

The boats are long gone; the lake is now a haven for wildfowl. Within these 127 acres (51ha) – the 'Golden Acre' name was as fanciful as 'the Blue Lagoon' – is a wide variety of wildlife habitats, from open heathland to an old quarry. Lovers of birds, trees and flowers will find plenty to interest them at every season of the year. One of the few echoes of the original Golden Acre Park is a café situated close to the entrance. Reflecting the park's increasing popularity, a large car park has been built on the opposite side of the main road, with pedestrian access to the park via a tunnel beneath the road. This intriguing park offers excellent walking, and wheelchair users, too, can make a circuit of the lake on a broad path.

Walk **39**

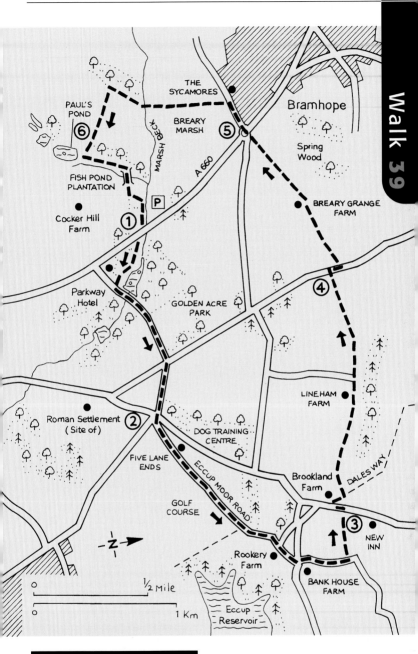

Walk 39 **Directions**

① From the far left end of the car park, take steps and an underpass beneath the road, into **Golden Acre Park**. Take one of the paths to the left or the right around the lake; at the far left end of the lake leave the park by a gate (signed '**Meanwood Valley Trail**'). Bear left, along a tree-lined path, to a T-junction of roads. Take the road ahead, up to the aptly-named **Five Lane Ends**.

Walk 39

② Take the second road on the left (**Eccup Moor Road**), passing a dog training centre on the left and a golf course on the right. Ignore side turnings till you reach the outbuildings of **Bank House Farm**, where you take a farm track to the left. It soon narrows to become a path between hedgerows. About 50yds (46m) before the footpath bears right take a stile in the fence on your left, to join a field path to a wall stile. Cross another field to meet a road (the **New Inn** is just along the road to your right).

WHERE TO EAT AND DRINK ⓘ

It requires the shortest of detours, at about the half-way point of this walk, to visit the **New Inn**, near Eccup. A sign welcomes walkers – as do the open fires and beer garden – and an extensive menu will whet your appetite.

---

cross a field to the bottom right-hand corner and another stile. Head left, across the next field, to a stile, that brings you out at the A660 by a roundabout.

⑤ Cross the main road and take **The Sycamores** ahead. After 250yds (230m) take a waymarked stile on the left to join a field-edge footpath with a hedge on the left. Cross a succession of five stiles, and then tiny Marsh Beck, before skirting an area of woodland on your right. Beyond a ladder stile you join a farm track, bearing left past a farmhouse to enter **Fish Pond Plantation** via a gate.

WHAT TO LOOK FOR ⓘ

Look for the damp-loving alder trees in Breary Marsh. Their seeds are designed to float on the water. During winter you should see little siskins (a type of finch) feeding on the seeds, of which they are particularly fond. You may also spy the vivid caterpillar of the alder moth.

---

③ Go left along the road for just 20yds (18m) to take a stile on your right (signposted 'Dales Way'), leading to a field path. After another stile you join a track ahead over a further stile and uphill with a wall to your left. Veer right across pasture to a wall stile and continue towards **Lineham Farm**. Beyond two more wall stiles you pass the farm buildings and join a good track. When the track goes left you keep straight ahead on a path between fences. After field-edge walking, and a further three stiles, you reach a road.

④ Go right along the road for 150yds (138m) and take a waymarked stile on the left by a gate. Follow the field-edge path with a fence on your left. Through two kissing gates bear left across a field, keeping to the right of **Breary Grange Farm**. After a ladder stile,

⑥ Bear right, through the wood, soon reaching the retaining wall of a small stretch of water known locally as **Paul's Pond**. Bear left here on a woodland path accompanying a stream. Having crossed the stream on a footbridge, you soon join a duckboarded walkway that keeps you dry-footed as you cross **Breary Marsh**. The walkway meanders back towards the underpass beneath the A660 road. Go left, in front of it, back into the car park.

WHILE YOU'RE THERE ⓘ

Take a look at Bramhope's **Puritan Chapel**, adjacent to the entrance to the Post House Hotel on the A660, as it passes through the village. This small, simple chapel was built in 1649, by devout Puritan Robert Dyneley. It contains original furnishings, including box pews and a three-deck pulpit.

Fairburn Ings and Ledsham

A visit to North Yorkshire's very own 'Lake District', now a bird reserve of national importance.

•DISTANCE•	5 miles (8km)
•MINIMUM TIME•	2hrs 30min
•ASCENT / GRADIENT•	131ft (40m) ▲ ▲ ▲
•LEVEL OF DIFFICULTY•	🚶 🚶🚶 🚶🚶
•PATHS•	Good paths and tracks (some newly-created from spoil heaps), 7 stiles
•LANDSCAPE•	Lakes, riverside and reclaimed colliery spoil heaps
•SUGGESTED MAP•	aqua3 OS Explorer 289 Leeds
•START / FINISH•	Grid reference: SE 472278
•DOG FRIENDLINESS•	Keep on lead around main lake, due to wildfowl
•PARKING•	Free parking in Cut Road, Fairburn. From A1, drive into village, turn left 100yds (91m) past Three Horseshoes pub,
•PUBLIC TOILETS•	Fairburn Ings visitor centre

BACKGROUND TO THE WALK

The coalfields of Yorkshire were most concentrated in the borough of Wakefield. Towns and villages grew up around the mines, and came to represent the epitome of northern industrial life. Mining was always a dangerous and dirty occupation, and it changed the landscape dramatically. Opencast mines swallowed up huge tracts of land, and the extensive spoil heaps were all-too-visible evidence of industry.

For the men of these communities, mining was almost the only work available. So when the industry went into decline, these communities were hit especially hard. Historians will look back at the mining industry and be amazed at the speed of this decline. Mines that were earmarked for expansion could be closed down a year or two later. To politicians of the left, the miners were sacrificial lambs; to those of the right, the miners exerted too much power. For good or ill the mining industry was decimated, and thousands of miners lost their livelihoods.

The death of the industry was emphasised by the closing down of Caphouse Colliery and its subsequent conversion into the National Coal Mining Museum for England. The spoil heaps that scarred the landscape are going back to nature, a process hastened by tree planting and other reclamation schemes. Opencast workings are being transformed into lakes and wetlands – valuable havens for wildfowl and migrating birds. Within a single generation parts of Yorkshire may have a network of lakes to rival the Norfolk Broads. In the meantime, these industrial wastelands are still rather scruffy. Not that the birds seem to mind...

Fairburn Ings Nature Reserve

Fairburn Ings, now under the stewardship of the Royal Society for the Protection of Birds (RSPB), was one of the earliest examples of colliery reclamation – being designated a Local Nature Reserve in 1957. The result is arguably the most important nature reserve in North

Yorkshire. The site seems rather unpromising; it's hemmed in by the A1, the conurbation of Castleford, the River Aire, a railway and old spoil heaps. Nevertheless, the stark outlines of the spoil heaps are now softened by banks of silver birches, and mining subsidence has created a broad expanse of water near the village of Fairburn, as well as smaller pools and flashes.

There are plenty of birds to be seen at all times of the year, though the numbers of ducks, geese, swans and gulls are at their highest during the winter months. The 600 acres (243ha) of wetlands are a magnet for birds during the spring and autumn migration. In summer there are many species of wildlife nesting on the scrapes and islands – including terns and a large, noisy colony of black-headed gulls. The best places from which to view all this activity are the public hides that overlook the lake.

Ledsham

Hidden away from the traffic hammering up and down the nearby A1, the estate village of Ledsham is a tranquil little backwater. Behind the Saxon church – one of the oldest in Yorkshire – is a row of picturesque almshouses. The Chequers Inn is an old and characterful country pub with, unusually, a six-day licence. Some 170 years ago, so the story goes, the one-time lady of the manor was on her way to church, when she saw some of her farm-hands in a drunken state. To avoid this happening in future, she decreed that Sundays in Ledsham should be 'dry'.

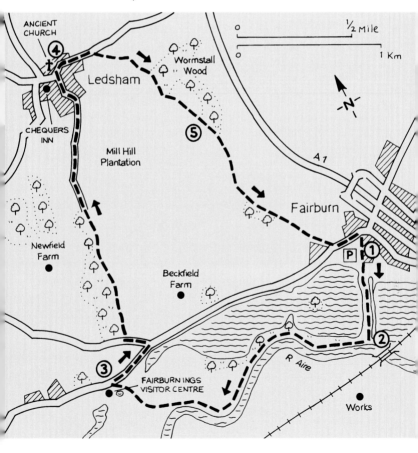

Walk 40 Directions

① Walk down **Cut Road** as it narrows to a track. Soon you have the main lake to your right, and a smaller stretch of water to your left. When the track forks, keep right (unless you want to visit the first of the bird hides, in which case detour to the left). The path finishes at the end of the lake, on approaching the **River Aire**.

WHERE TO EAT AND DRINK

The **Chequers Inn** in Ledsham harks back to the past in more ways than one. The exposed beams and open fires give the pub a homely atmosphere. Excellent food makes the place popular for lunches with walkers and locals. Closed on Sundays.

② Go right here, to join a path along the top of a ridge (actually an old spoil heap), with the river to your left and the lake right. Look out for a couple of other bird hides, before you lose sight of the lake. The path crosses a broader expanse of spoil heap, through scrubland, following the river in a broad arc to the right, before descending to a stile above another small mere. Bear right on a broad track and drop down into the car park of the **Fairburn Ings visitor centre**.

WHILE YOU'RE THERE

There's a mixture of old and new at **Ferrybridge**, where the M62 crosses the A1. When travellers from the south and east reach this point, and see the huge cooling towers of Ferrybridge Power Station, they know they have arrived in West Yorkshire. But adjacent to the motorway bridge is a surprising anachronism: an 18th-century bridge by the Yorkshire architect John Carr, better known for his work on Harewood House.

③ Meet a road. Go right for 100yds (91m), then go left (signed '**Ledston and Kippax**') for just 100yds (91m), and pick up a path on your right that hugs the right-hand fringe of a wood. Beyond the wood, take a path between fields; it broadens to a track as you approach the village of **Ledsham**. At a new estate of houses, turn right, along **Manor Garth**.

④ You arrive in the village by the ancient church. Walk right, along the road (or, for refreshments, go left to the **Chequers Inn**). Beyond the village, where the road bears left, take a gate on the right, giving access to a good track uphill. Where the main track goes right, into fields, continue along a track ahead, into woodland. Leave the wood by a stile, crossing pasture on a grassy track. Two stiles take you across a narrow spur of woodland.

⑤ Head slightly left, uphill, across the next field, to follow a fence and hedgerow. Continue – soon on a better track – across a stile. Beyond the next stile the track bears left, towards farm buildings: but you keep straight on, with a fence on your right, along the field path. Through a metal gate, join an access track downhill. Go left, when you meet the road, and back into the village of **Fairburn**.

WHAT TO LOOK FOR

Be sure to take a pair of binoculars with you. Fairburn Ings is a bird reserve of national importance and, especially during the spring and autumn migrations, all kinds of rare birds can be seen. There are a number of strategically sited hides along this walk, from which you can watch the birds without disturbing them. Watch especially for the rare but inconspicuous gadwall, pochard and golden plover.

The Gorgeous Grounds of Allen Banks

Walking through a wooded gorge to Dickie's watchtower.

•DISTANCE•	5 miles (8km)
•MINIMUM TIME•	2hrs 45min
•ASCENT / GRADIENT•	420ft (128m) ▲ ▲ ▲
•LEVEL OF DIFFICULTY•	🚶🚶 🚶🚶 🚶
•PATHS•	Well-signposted woodland paths, 7 stiles
•LANDSCAPE•	Wooded river valley
•SUGGESTED MAP•	aqua3 OS Explorer OL43 Hadrian's Wall
•START / FINISH•	Grid reference: NY 798640
•DOG FRIENDLINESS•	Dogs should be under close control
•PARKING•	Car park included in fee for walk (Note below)
•PUBLIC TOILETS•	At car park
•NOTE•	Early part of walk is not right of way, National Trust makes small charge per adult to walk here

BACKGROUND TO THE WALK

After having an easy youth in the high Northumbrian moors and dales, the East and West Allen rivers join forces at Cupola. There's only 4 miles (6.4km) to go as the crow flies to get to the wide lazy waters of the South Tyne, but the Allen will be put through its paces as the hills in the east and west close in. Even in the last stretch the river has to squeeze through a tight gorge between Ridley Common and Morralee Fell. This is known as Allen Banks and has, for centuries, been cloaked with thick woodland – a spot of great beauty.

Designing the Grounds

Allen Banks was part of the Ridley Hall Estate, whose history goes back to medieval times when the Ridley family presided here. The original hall was destroyed by a great fire in the middle of the 18th century and the magnificent sandstone mansion you see today is Georgian. John Davidson of Otterburn purchased the estate in the 1830s for his wife Susan, granddaughter of the 9th Earl of Strathmore. In those times the valley was mined for both coal and lead. Susan Davidson took a keen interest in the grounds and not only laid out the formal gardens, but designed a network of paths through the wilder environs of the riverside and woods. The Davidsons were childless, and on their deaths the estate passed to John Bowes and his French wife, Josephine. It was the Bowes-Lyon family who gave Allen Banks to the National Trust in 1942.

Nature Reserve

Beyond the car park, which is sited on the hall's old kitchen garden, the hills close in, with Raven Crag towering above to the right and Morralee Fell on the far banks to the left. The river bends to the right and soon you enter the nature reserve at Briarwood Banks. After Plankey Mill the route climbs out of the valley and comes across the crumbling remains of

Staward Pele. This 14th-century fortified house was once owned by the Dukes of York and leased to the monks of Hexham. Later it fell into the hands of Dickie of Kingswood, a local character and petty criminal. Although today the old house is tangled with scrub, in better times it would have had a commanding view of the valley and any invading border reivers. In Dickie's case, the police wouldn't have been confident about carrying out a successful raid if he had been suspected of any wrongdoing.

Walk 41

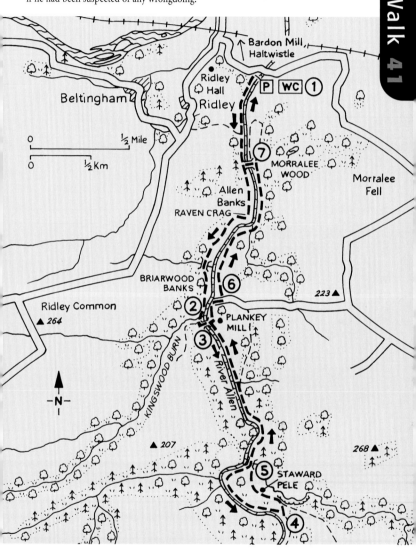

Walk 41 Directions

① Follow the riverside path from the back of the car park and stay with the lower left fork where the

path divides. Stay on the Allen's west banks rather than crossing the suspension bridge. Beyond it the path tucks beneath **Raven Crag**. The river bends to the right and you soon enter the nature reserve at

Walk 41

Briarwod Banks. Here the ancient woodland has seen continuous growth dating back to the end of the last ice age, some 10,000 years ago. With broadleaved trees like sessile oak, wych elm, ash, birch, rowan and alder flourishing this is a haven for wildlife, and over 60 species of bird have been recorded in the valley. These include the sparrowhawk, tawny owl, wood warbler, woodcock and song thrush.

② On Briarwood Banks the path uses a footbridge across **Kingswood Burn**, then turns left to cross the suspension bridge across the **Allen**. You are now at **Plankey Mill**.

③ Turn right along the field-edge path close to the river and go over either of two step stiles back into woodland. If you chose the riverside stile some steps will lead you back to the main track. You are now

following the green waymarks of the **Staward Pele path** which stays close to the river, though it's often high above the banks. Just beyond a footbridge the path divides. Take the right fork – the left is your downhill return route.

④ On reaching the top eastern edge of the woods the path turns left where it first passes the gatehouse of **Staward Pele** then the ruins of the fortified farm itself.

⑤ Beyond the pele the track descends, steeply, sometimes in steps back to the previously mentioned footbridge. Retrace your steps to **Plankey Mill**.

⑥ On reaching the tarred lane by the mill, turn right, go uphill along it, then, at a sharp bend, turn off it on to an enclosed footpath. This leads to a another footpath that follows a field edge alongside the river's east bank.

⑦ Turn left over the suspension bridge opposite the **Morralee Wood** turn off, then turn right along the outward footpath back to the car park.

The Wild Cattle of Chillingham

A walk that encircles a haunted castle and the home of the only wild cattle left in Britain.

•DISTANCE•	6 miles (9.7km)
•MINIMUM TIME•	3hrs
•ASCENT / GRADIENT•	754ft (230m) ▲▲▲
•LEVEL OF DIFFICULTY•	林林林
•PATHS•	Hill track, surfaced road
•LANDSCAPE•	Hill, arable and woodland
•SUGGESTED MAP•	aqua3 OS Explorer 340 Holy Island & Bamburgh
•START / FINISH•	Grid reference: NU 071248
•DOG FRIENDLINESS•	Dogs not allowed in Chillingham Wood, even on lead
•PARKING•	Forest car park at Hepburn Wood
•PUBLIC TOILETS•	None on route

BACKGROUND TO THE WALK

The origins of the Chillingham wild cattle are not known. Their skull structure suggests similarities with the aurochs, so they may be descended from those ancient wild oxen that once roamed Britain. Recent DNA tests performed on dead animals show that they are unrelated to any other European cattle. Having remained uncontaminated by outside stock, they are probably the only genetically pure cattle in the world. They are always white, no coloured animals have ever been born, and they are definitely wild.

Captured Cattle
The Chillingham herd has roamed its 365-acre (148ha) park for almost 700 years, since Sir Thomas Percy was granted a royal licence to fortify Chillingham Castle and enclose the grounds. The captured cattle may have provided a food supply. Over the years they have never been domesticated. The strongest bull leads the herd, he remains 'King', and sires all the calves born during his 'rule' until such time as another bull successfully challenges him. Even a birth is accompanied by a ritual, which must be observed before the new calf is accepted into the herd.

Care of the Herd
The number of cattle in the herd normally varies from 40 to 60, but during the severe winter of 1947, their numbers fell to 13. Their wild nature meant that normal agricultural methods could not be employed to help them. The Chillingham cattle never seek shelter other than in the surrounding trees and will eat only grass and hay and, even when starving, will not accept oats or prepared cattle food. Fortunately the cattle are rarely ill, but when disease does strike, they cannot be approached by a vet. The tragic outbreak of foot and mouth disease in 1967 and again in 2001 threatened the survival of the herd, on the earlier occasion encroaching within 2 miles (3.2km) of Chillingham.

The Chillingham Wild Cattle Association was formed in 1939 to look after the welfare of the herd. The 8th Earl of Tankerville bequeathed ownership of the herd to the association on his death in 1971. When the 9th earl died in 1980, the Chillingham Estate was put up for sale. As a result of the intervention of the Duke of Northumberland, Chillingham Park was sold separately from the castle to the Sir James Knott Charitable Trust, which granted the association grazing rights for 999 years.

Visitors can see the cattle in their natural surroundings, which look much as they did in medieval times. The cattle's behaviour, however, is unpredictable, so for safety reasons, you can only enter the park when accompanied by the warden. Binoculars are recommended for a close view. The park is open daily except Tuesday and the entrance fee is relatively modest.

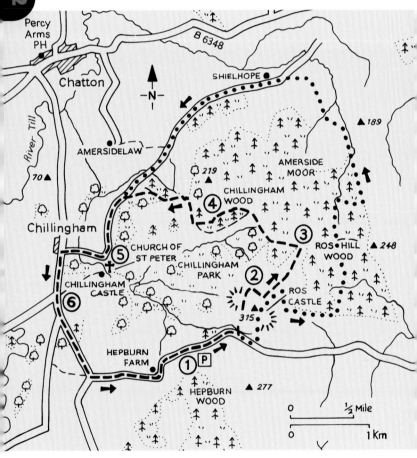

Walk 42 **Directions**

① On leaving the car park, turn right on to the road and go uphill for ½ mile (800m) and round a bend to a National Trust notice

indicating Ros Castle. Follow the track to a gate in the wall to your left and go through the gate into **Chillingham Wood**. Turn right, then left and follow marker posts on to a broader track after 100yds (90m). This leads you uphill, then

Walk **42**

across a level stretch to a fence. On your left is a view over Chillingham Park, where you might, on occasion, be able to see the wild cattle.

② Turn right at the fence and go uphill as indicated by the signpost to Chillingham. When you reach the wall, turn left and follow the track between the wall and the fence to a picnic table. Continue to the next forest, and walk between the wall and the forest for about 250yds (229m) to the next signpost to Chillingham.

③ Turn left and descend through the forest, following the marker posts about 50yds (46m) apart. When this small track reaches a junction with a track signed 'Forest Way', turn right and continue to a signpost pointing to Amerside Moor and Chillingham. Take the Chillingham direction, through two tall kissing gates to a picnic area with two tables.

④ Continue along the track to a forest road and turn right on to this, which becomes metalled lower down. When you reach a sign pointing left over a small bridge to the Forest Walk, ignore this and instead go through the gate and along the road out of the forest. The road you are now on leads to the entrance to **Chillingham Park**.

⑤ Follow the road past the **Church of St Peter**, on your left, then past a gate leading to **Chillingham Castle**. Cross the **Hollow Burn** either by ford or footbridge and continue to a T-junction with the main road. Turn left and follow the road, passing the main castle gate after 550yds (500m).

⑥ At the next fork in the road, take the left fork and go uphill to the crossroads. This road is not very busy with traffic and has good grass verges for walking on. Turn left on to the road to **Hepburn Farm**. Follow this, past the farm buildings, and continue to **Hepburn Wood** car park.

Caerlaverock Castle and the Solway Merses

A ramble taking in an ancient fortress and a National Nature Reserve.

•DISTANCE•	5¼ miles (8.4km)
•MINIMUM TIME•	2hrs 30min
•ASCENT / GRADIENT•	82ft (25m) ▲ ▲ ▲
•LEVEL OF DIFFICULTY•	🚶🚶 🚶 🚶🚶
•PATHS•	Country lanes, farm tracks and salt marsh, 1 stile
•LANDSCAPE•	Pastures, salt marsh, riverside and hills
•SUGGESTED MAP•	aqua3 OS Explorer 314 Solway Firth
•START / FINISH•	Grid reference: NY 051656
•DOG FRIENDLINESS•	Keep on lead while on reserve
•PARKING•	Car park at Wildfowl and Wetlands Trust Reserve
•PUBLIC TOILETS•	At Wildfowl and Wetlands Trust Reserve

BACKGROUND TO THE WALK

Against the impressive backdrop of Criffel, guarded by the wide waters of the Solway Firth, the salt marshes and the impressive medieval castle of Caerlaverock, this out-of-the-way corner of Scotland is a haven for wildlife and a treasure trove of history

A Castle Under Siege

Caerlaverock, the Castle of the Lark, was once the main gatekeeper to south west Scotland. Protected by mudflats and the shifting channels of the sea, it was vulnerable only from the landward side. During the Scottish Wars of Independence (1286–1370) it was attacked frequently. From the siege of Caerlaverock by Edward I in 1300 through to the 17th century it was continually besieged, levelled and rebuilt. Its garrison last surrendered in 1640 after holding a Scottish army of Covenanters for over three months. Partially demolished, it crumbled to an ivy-covered ruin until restoration in the mid-20th century. Within the ruined walls of this triangular fortress, conservators continue their work on one of the finest Renaissance residences in Scotland.

Preserving the Balance

Conservation work of a different kind takes place on the merse (salt marsh) that bounds the Solway coast. Here Scottish Natural Heritage (SNH), the Wildfowl and Wetlands Trust (WWT) and the Caerlaverock Estate work at preserving the delicate balance that allows farming and wild fowling to exist alongside a National Nature Reserve.

The desolate open spaces, unchanged for centuries, echo to the cry of the wild geese in winter, the oystercatcher and heron in summer and the mating chorus of the natterjack toad in spring. But it wasn't always so. Wildfowling had seriously reduced the goose population to a few hundred in 1957, when the local landowner, the Duke of Norfolk, agreed to divide the merse into an area for controlled shooting and a wildlife sanctuary, now the National Nature Reserve. This is also one of the last places in Britain where scientists can study the natural processes of growth and erosion of salt marshes.

Sir Peter Scott

In 1970 the duke offered the naturalist, Sir Peter Scott, the lease of Eastpark Farm for the WWT. Here, every October, the Spitsbergen population of barnacle geese fly in from Norway to their winter quarters along the merse. The birds can be seen from specially constructed hides along roads shielded with high hedges to minimise disturbance to wildlife.

Whooper swans overwinter here too, along with the pink-footed goose, pintail, scaup, oystercatcher, knot, bar-tailed godwit, curlew and redshank. Staff at Eastpark organise a variety of events to help visitors appreciate the reserve, including birdwatching, natterjack toad and bat spotting and pond dipping. As part of the conservation process, wildfowling is permitted in winter. Barnacle geese are protected but other species are fair game. The wildfowlers are experts at recognition and the SNH wardens ensure fair play.

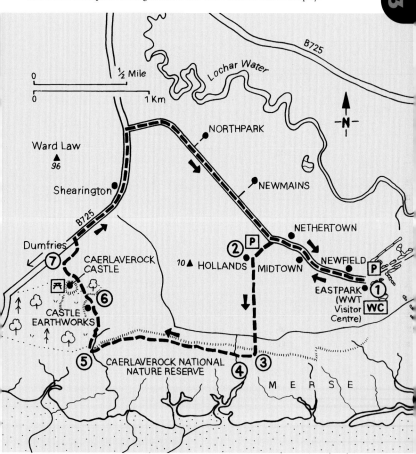

Walk 43 **Directions**

① Exit the car park and turn right on to a farm road. Follow this past the farms of **Newfield** and **Midtown** then turn left and go past

a bungalow and some houses. Just before the farm of **Hollands** there is a waymarker pointing to a car park, on the right, and straight ahead for walks. Go straight ahead, continue to the farm steading and turn left.

Walk 43

② Go through a gate and on to a farm track. This stretches away into the distance and has high hedges on both sides. Continue along this track between the hedges and on, over an overgrown section, until you reach a fence. Cross this by a stile and turn right at the signpost indicating **Caerlaverock National Nature Reserve**.

③ A sign here informs visitors that regulated wildfowling (shooting) takes place between 1 September and 20 February. Follow the rough track through the grass along the edge of the merse in the direction of the arrow on the footpath waymarker post. The path can be very boggy at all times and the grass will be high in summer.

> **WHERE TO EAT AND DRINK** ℹ
> There's an excellent, newly opened family-friendly café and tea room in the visitors' centre at **Eastpark**. It is bright and spacious and serves a good range of hot food and beverages, snacks and cakes. It also houses the WWT gift and bookshop.

④ Cross a small wooden bridge, an electric fence covered with a piece of insulated piping and another small bridge. The path splits at several points and meanders back and forth but all the lines of the path rejoin and you'll end up at the same place which ever one you take.

⑤ Eventually a tumbledown wire and post fence will appear on the right-hand side. Follow this fence towards a wood, passing through an overgrown area and then bear right, through a gate and into a field. Walk to the left around the perimeter of this field, past some cottages, and then turn left through

> **WHILE YOU'RE THERE** ℹ
> The **Dumfries Museum and Camera Obscura** is housed in a former windmill and has a comprehensive collection covering the history of the region, its people and wildlife. Here you'll see fossils, stone carvings by early Christians, a range of Victoriana, some death masks, a plaster cast of the skull of Robert Burns and the first writings of J M Barrie who who lived in Dumfries for a time.

a gate to emerge on to a farm track, passing a sign pointing the way for **Caerlaverock Castle** and into the castle grounds.

⑥ Follow the road past the old castle, which has been excavated and has information boards to explain the ruins, and go through a wood with nature trail information boards to **Caerlaverock Castle**. There is a children's playground, a siege machine and picnic tables around the ramparts of the castle.

⑦ At the far end go through an arch and continue to the T-junction with a country lane. Turn right and continue for about a mile (1.6km) then turn right on to another lane signposted 'Wildfowl and Wetlands Reserve'. Continue on this road past the farms of **Northpark**, **Newmains** and **Nethertown** and then back to the car park at **Eastpark**.

> **WHAT TO LOOK FOR** ℹ
> While on the salt marsh and mudflats section of this walk the large hill immediately in front of you is Criffel. Look out along here for **grebes** and wintering **goldeneye** and in the spring for the **black-tailed godwit** on passage. In spring and summer this area is particularly rich in **wild flowers**. You'll need to carry a field guide with you to get the most from the walk.

A Windy Walk to St Abb's Head

A refreshing wildlife walk along the cliffs.

•**DISTANCE**•	4 miles (6.4km)
•**MINIMUM TIME**•	1hr 30min
•**ASCENT / GRADIENT**•	443ft (135m) ▲▲▲
•**LEVEL OF DIFFICULTY**•	🚶 🚶 🚶
•**PATHS**•	Clear footpaths and established tracks
•**LANDSCAPE**•	Dramatic cliff tops and lonely lighthouse
•**SUGGESTED MAP**•	aqua3 OS Explorer 346 Berwick-upon-Tweed
•**START / FINISH**•	Grid reference: NT 913674
•**DOG FRIENDLINESS**•	They'll love the fresh air, but keep on lead by cliffs
•**PARKING**•	At visitor centre
•**PUBLIC TOILETS**•	At visitor centre

BACKGROUND TO THE WALK

St Abb's Head is one of those places that people forget to visit. You only ever seem to hear it mentioned on the shipping forecast – and its name is generally followed by a rather chilly outlook – along the lines of 'north easterly five, continuous light drizzle, poor'. In fact you could be forgiven for wondering if it even exists or is simply a mysterious expanse of sea – like Dogger, Fisher or German Bight.

But St Abb's Head does exist, as you'll find out on this lovely windswept walk which will rumple your hair and leave the salty tang of the sea lingering on your lips. The dramatic cliffs, along which you walk to reach the lonely lighthouse, form an ideal home for thousands of nesting seabirds as they provide superb protection from mammalian predators. Birds you might spot on this walk include guillemots, razorbills, kittiwakes, herring gulls, shags and fulmars – as well as a few puffins.

Guillemots and razorbills are difficult to differentiate, as they're both black and white, and have an upright stance – rather like small, perky penguins. However, you should be able to spot the difference if you've got binoculars as razorbills have distinctive blunt beaks. Both birds belong to the auk family, the most famous member of which is probably the great auk, which went the way of the dodo and became extinct in 1844 – a victim of the contemporary passion for egg collecting.

Luckily no egg collector could scale these cliffs, which are precipitous and surrounded by treacherous seas. Do this walk in the nesting season (May to July) and you may well see young birds jumping off the high cliff ledge into the open sea below. Even though they can't yet fly, as their wings are little more than stubs, the baby birds are nevertheless excellent swimmers and have a better chance of survival in the water than in their nests – where they could fall prey to marauding gulls. Neither razorbills nor guillemots are particularly agile in the air, but they swim with the ease of seals, using their wings and feet to propel and steer their sleek little bodies as they fish beneath the waves.

While the steep cliffs are home to most of the seabirds round St Abb's Head, the low, flat rocks below are also used by wildlife, as they are the favoured nesting site of shags. These large black birds are almost indistinguishable from cormorants – except for the distinctive crest on their heads that gives them a quizzical appearance. They tend to fly low over the water – in contrast to the graceful fulmars that frequently soar along the cliff tops as you walk, hitching a ride on convenient currents of air.

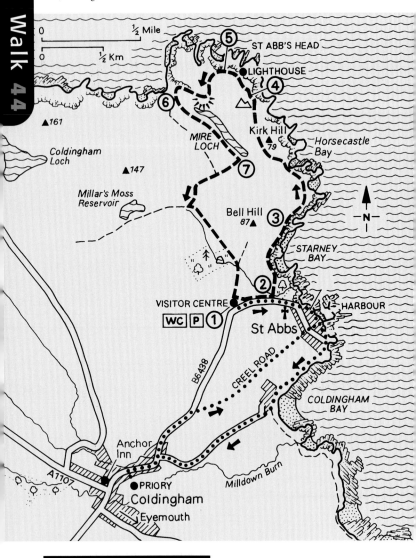

Walk 44 Directions

① From the car park, take the path that runs past the information board and the play area. Walk past the **visitor centre**, then take the footpath on the left, parallel to the main road. At the end of the path turn left and go through a kissing gate – you'll immediately get great views of the sea.

② Follow the track, pass the sign to Starney Bay and continue, passing fields on your left-hand side. Your

Walk 44

track now winds around the edge of the bay – to your right is the little harbour at St Abbs. The track then winds around the cliff edge, past dramatic rock formations and eventually to some steps.

③ Walk down the steps, then follow the grassy track as it bears left, with a fence on the left. Go up a slope, over a stile and maintain direction on the obvious grassy track. The path soon veers away from the cliff edge, past high ground on the right, then runs up a short, steep slope to a crossing of tracks.

④ Maintain direction by taking the left-hand track which runs up a slope. You'll soon get great views of the **St Abb's Head lighthouse** ahead, dramatically situated on the cliff's edge. Continue to the lighthouse and walk in front of the lighthouse buildings and down to join a tarmac road.

⑤ Follow this road which takes you away from the cliff edge. Continue to an obvious bend, from where you get your first views of the

Mire Loch below. You now follow the path downhill to the right, to reach a cattle grid.

⑥ Turn left here to pick up the narrow track by the loch, with the wall on your right-hand side. It's pretty overgrown at the start so can be hard to find, but it soon becomes much more obvious. Walk beside the loch and continue until you reach a gate.

⑦ Turn right along the wide track and walk up to the road. Go left now and continue to cross a cattle grid. When you reach a bend in the road, follow the tarmac track as it bears left. You'll soon go through a gate, then pass some cottages before reaching the car park on the left-hand side.

Walk 45

The Great Forest of Loch Ard

One of Scotland's great woodlands, hiding place of the Stone of Destiny and birthplace of the Scottish Parliament.

•DISTANCE•	3½ miles (5.7km)
•MINIMUM TIME•	2hrs
•ASCENT / GRADIENT•	98ft (30m)
•LEVEL OF DIFFICULTY•	
•PATHS•	Roads, forest roads and trails
•LANDSCAPE•	Fields, hills, forest and loch
•SUGGESTED MAP•	aqua3 OS Explorer 365 The Trossachs
•START / FINISH•	Grid reference: NS 521009
•DOG FRIENDLINESS•	Keep under control or on lead to avoid disturbing wildlife
•PARKING•	Car park at Aberfoyle beside tourist office in centre of town
•PUBLIC TOILETS•	Beside tourist office next to car park

BACKGROUND TO THE WALK

L ying between the town of Aberfoyle and the foothills of Ben Lomond this huge area of woodland is part of the Queen Elizabeth Forest Park. It stretches from just north of Drymen almost to the banks of Loch Katrine. It may look like just another conifer plantation but a walk through any part of it will reveal a surprising variety of landscapes, flora and fauna.

Forestry Management
Most of the forested land was purchased by the Forestry Commission in the early 1930s. It was planted straight away and by the closing years of the century consisted of mature woodland. Ongoing thinning started in the 1950s and areas were felled towards the end of the century. Some 60,000 tons of timber are extracted each year from the park as a whole. With the United Kingdom currently importing about 90 per cent of its timber needs, the increase in harvesting the park's mature trees will help to reduce this figure.

The area south of Lochan Spling was initially planted with Norway spruce, Sitka spruce, larch and Scots pine. Most of the spruce together with some of the larch and pine was felled in the 1980s and replaced with Douglas fir, larch and Sitka spruce. But native broadleaves have been planted too, including 10,000 oak trees to augment the remains of the ancient oak woods that once covered most of the area. Birch and rowan have been regenerating naturally. Part of this area has been left to mature to provide magnificent specimens the equal of anything in European forests. The entire area is enclosed within a deer fence to let the trees have a chance to establish.

Wilderness Areas
Wildlife is abundant, including red squirrels and capercaillie. Decaying pines, which have been uprooted in gales or just collapsed, support wood boring insects and provide a ready food supply for a whole host of birds. There are peat bogs and wilderness areas like the one

just south of Duchray water in the old wood of Drumore. Here there are no trails, but amidst this jungle-like habitat can be found blueberry, chickweed, wintergreen, cow-wheat and cowberry. You will probably see some evidence of red and roe deer and if you are really quiet may see rare birds like blackcock and woodpecker.

Changing attitudes to conservation and forestry management have helped to bring about a gradual reshaping of the forest to provide a more diverse range of tree species, a wider range of habitats and an environment rich in wildlife.

Stop at the Covenanters Inn where the Nationalists, led by John McCormick, met in 1949 to launch a petition, which they called the Second Covenant. The signatories called on the government of the day to give Scotland a devolved parliament. Over 2 million people signed the petition but it was not until the closing years of the 20th century, and after much argument, campaigning and voting, that their wishes were granted.

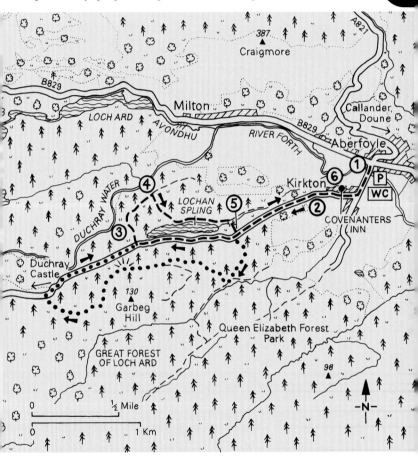

Walk 45 Directions

① Leave from the west end of the car park and turn left into **Manse Road**. Cross a narrow bridge over the **River Forth** (the river has its source near here although it is more usually associated with Edinburgh) and continue along the grass beside the road until the first junction on the right. Turn right here and head

Walk 45

uphill, passing the **Covenanters Inn**. A short distance past here is open countryside and the start of the Great Forest of Loch Ard.

② Head straight on along the forest road, keeping an ear open for heavy timber lorries. During the week this can get fairly busy, as this is a main forestry extraction route, so keep well into the side. After approximately ½ mile (800m) you will reach a staggered crossroads. Continue straight ahead along the forest road until you come to a turning on the right with a yellow waymarker. Turn right here.

③ Follow this waymarked trail through the forest almost to the banks of **Duchray Water**. This rises on the north face of Ben Lomond and joins with the Avondhu from Loch Ard to create the River Forth near Aberfoyle. The path curves right, continues to descend slightly and then reaches a junction.

④ Turn right and follow the path through the trees to the north banks of **Lochan Spling**. The path then swings left and, at the end of the Lochan, turns right at a waymarker pole, crosses a small stream and heads slightly uphill.

⑤ When the path reaches the T-junction, turn left and rejoin the main forest access road continuing along it to the **Covenanters Inn**. This takes its name not from the activities of the 17th-century Scottish Presbyterians, who were persecuted by the Stuart monarchy for refusing to give up their faith, but to the activities of 20th-century Scottish Nationalists.

⑥ Continue past the inn, where a later group of Nationalists temporarily hid Scotland's Stone of Destiny when it was liberated from Westminster Abbey in 1950, then turn left on to **Manse Road** at the junction and return to the start.

Moorland on Morrone

The hill at the back of Braemar gives a taste of the wildlife of the Cairngorms.

•DISTANCE•	6¾ miles (10.9km)
•MINIMUM TIME•	4hrs 15min
•ASCENT / GRADIENT•	2,000ft (610m) ▲▲▲
•LEVEL OF DIFFICULTY•	🏃 🏃 🏃
•PATHS•	Well-made but fairly steep path, track, 1 stile
•LANDSCAPE•	Rolling heather hills
•SUGGESTED MAP•	aqua3 OS Explorer 387 Glen Shee & Braemar
•START / FINISH•	Grid reference: NO 143911
•DOG FRIENDLINESS•	On leads in reserve, also on hill during grouse nesting May/June
•PARKING•	Duck Pond, at top of Chapel Brae, Braemar
•PUBLIC TOILETS•	Braemar centre (opposite Fife Arms)

BACKGROUND TO THE WALK

Coming down the back of Morrone Hill, you descend through several different plant zones, and the home ground of two distinctive Grampian birds.

Ptarmigan Pterritory

On the windswept, often snow-covered summit plateau, gravel alternates with shrubby plants that grow barely ankle-high. These are food for the ptarmigan, a bird of the grouse family that's rather like a small hen. Uniquely among British birds it turns white in the winter, and in spring and early summer it will still be white in patches. Its late summer plumage is paler than the grouse, and more speckled. But the easy way to recognise it is by where it lives – a grouse above the heather line is a ptarmigan – and by its behaviour. It relies on camouflage, and when you notice it, will probably be standing on the gravel only a few yards away. Even then, it doesn't fly away, but will probably wander off round the back of a boulder. In springtime, the male bird's soaring display flight is accompanied by a soundtrack of belches and cackles. The 'P' at the beginning of its name is purely ornamental – in Gaelic it's tarmachan.

Heather and Grouse

At the 2,000ft (610m) mark, bilberry and some grass grow, along with dwarf heather. Once you turn down on to slightly more sheltered ground, the heather springs up twice as high. At around 1,500ft (457m), it is deep enough to hinder off-path walking. Wild flowers like yellow tormentil and white woodruff are established, and you may see meadow pipits and mountain hare.

A small brown bird – or more likely three or four – leaps up out of the heather with a squawking cry that seems to say 'go back, go back!' Grouse go with heather, like pandas go with bamboo and koalas with gum trees. Red grouse are found only in the British Isles, and unfortunately their heather country, however familiar and tiresome to Scottish walkers, is rare and vanishing in a world context. The grouse need old leggy heather to nest in, but shorter, younger plants to eat. As a result, grouse moors are burnt in a ten-year cycle to provide tall heather with short fresh heather near by. The piebald effect of 'muirburn', as it's called, gives these lumpy hills an attractive extra texture.

Eighty per cent of the grouse's diet is heather, the rest being the insects that live in it. As birds lack teeth they require small stones in their gizzards to help grind their food up and aid digestion. For grouse, sharp quartz grit is ideal, and you may spot small piles of this beside the track.

Walk 46 Directions

① Take the wide track uphill, to the right of the duck pond at the top of **Chapel Brae**, bearing left twice to **Woodhill house**. The house can be bypassed by taking a small footpath on the right which rejoins the track just above. When the track forks again, bear left to a viewpoint indicator.

② Cross a track diagonally to a hill path marked 'Morrone'. The path has been rebuilt with rough stone steps. Higher up, it slants to the right along a line of rocky outcrops, a geological dyke of harder rock. At the top of this it turns directly uphill, passing five sprawling cairns. These are the turning point in the Morrone Hill Race that is part of the Braemar Games. The wide, stony path runs up to the **radio mast** and other ugly constructions on the summit.

WHERE TO EAT AND DRINK ℹ

The Duke of Fife used to own all Braemar west of the River Clunie. 'He is immensely rich,' said Queen Victoria with approval when he wanted to marry her daughter. The **Fife Arms**, with the standard hewn pine trunks along its frontage, has a large bar full of hillwalkers (and their dogs, on leads). Bar meals are served in walker-size portions.

---

③ The summit, if you turn your back on the buildings, has fine views across Deeside to the high Cairngorms. On the main tops, Ben Macdui and Beinn a' Bhuird, snow may show right through the summer. To the east you will see Loch Callater and the White Mounth plateau. A notable hump is Cac Carn Beag, one of the summits of Lochnagar. Morrone's summit area is bare stones, but if you go past the buildings you'll find the start of a wide track. It runs down to a shallow col and climbs to the cairn on the low summit beyond. Here it bends left towards a lower col, but before reaching it, turns left again down the side of the hill. A gentle zig-zagging descent leads to the road by the **Clunie Water**.

④ Turn left, alongside the river, for 1½ miles (2.4km). Ben Avon with its row of summit tors fills the skyline ahead. After a snow gate and golf clubhouse comes a road sign warning of a cattle grid (the grid itself is round the next bend). Here a track, back up to the left, has a blue-topped waymarker pole.

⑤ Go up between caravans to a ladder stile with dog flap. A faint path leads up under birches, bearing right and becoming clearer. After a gate in a fence the path becomes quite clear, leading to a Scottish Natural Heritage signboard and blue waymarker at the top of the birchwood. The path becomes a track with a fence on its right and, in 220yds (201m), reaches the viewpoint indicator, Point ②. From here you can make your return to the duck pond.

WHAT TO LOOK FOR ℹ

The tundra shrubs that grow on the plateau belong to the heather family, but with oval leaves rather than needles. They can be distinguished easily from August as their berries are conveniently colour-coded. The **crowberry** fruit is black, the **cowberry** red and the **bilberry**, also known as whortleberry and blaeberry, has a juicy purple fruit and pale green leaves. Ptarmigan droppings are stained purple with this fruit, which is also tasty to humans.

WHILE YOU'RE THERE ℹ

Braemar Castle is smaller, older and to my eye much more attractive than Balmoral, where the Queen lives. It was an important strong point, replacing the even older ruin alongside the River Clunie just above the bridge. Its surrounding wall is a later improvement, designed to cope with attackers during the age of the musket. Inside it has the world's largest cairngorm (a semi-precious stone), and underneath there's a pit dungeon for miscreants.

Around the Small Shepherd

Two valley passes through the high mountains at the head of Glen Coe.

•DISTANCE•	8 miles (12.9km)
•MINIMUM TIME•	4hrs 30min
•ASCENT / GRADIENT•	1,300ft (396m) ▲▲▲
•LEVEL OF DIFFICULTY•	👫 👫 👫
•PATHS•	Rough, unmade paths, some boggy bits, no stiles
•LANDSCAPE•	Remote high valleys into heart of hills
•SUGGESTED MAP•	aqua3 OS Explorer 384 Glen Coe & Glen Etive
•START / FINISH•	Grid reference: NN 213559
•DOG FRIENDLINESS•	Good, some streams to cross
•PARKING•	Large parking area on south side of A82, marked by yellow AA phone post
•PUBLIC TOILETS•	Glencoe village
•NOTE•	Fords in Lairig Eilde can be impassible or dangerous after heavy rain

BACKGROUND TO THE WALK

This walk uses two through routes on either side of Buachaille Etive Beag, the Small Herdsman of Etive. The Gaelic word 'Lairig' means a valley pass through the mountains. We use Lairig Gartain for the outward journey, and Lairig Eilde for the return, with a final link along the old Glen Coe road.

Passing Deer

This land is owned by the National Trust for Scotland, and there hasn't been any deer stalking for 65 years. When working on this book, I came across three hinds at the roadside car park. And one October I came through Lairig Eilde (Pass of the Deer) when its mountain walls were echoing with the roaring of the stags. It's an unforgettable sound – rather like a lion, but a little like a cow too.

For most of the year the hinds gather in small family groups with their calves of the last two years, while the stags go around in loose gangs. Deer dislike midges as much as humans do, so in summer they'll be on the high tops, though they may come down at night or in bad weather. In winter they'll be in the valley bottom or even at the roadside.

The calves are born in early June; they are dappled to camouflage them on the forest floor, which is their natural home. Within a few days they're running with the herd. The grace and speed of a week-old deer calf across a peat bog is the envy of any human hillwalker.

Getting into the Rut

The hinds have no antlers. The stags lose theirs in early summer and grow new ones ready for the rut: the September mating season. Large, many-branched antlers do not make a stag a better fighter, and are a serious drain on his system. They have probably evolved as display items, for intimidating other males and attracting females. A mighty roar may gain the stag the harem of a dozen hinds that he's after. If not, a quick clash of antlers will usually settle the matter. These displays are a way of determining which stag would have won without putting either to the risk of injury. However, the stag is sometimes prepared to fight for his wives and such fights can end in the death of one or even both males.

Kind to Be Cruel

Red deer owe their widespread survival in Scotland to the men who preserved and nurtured them in order to hunt them every autumn. For ancient aristocrats and newly rich Victorian manufacturers, the sport of sneaking up on a stag with a rifle was exciting, virile and also impressively expensive. With no predators, deer must still be culled by shooting, even on NTS land where no sport stalking takes place. Such culling will be done at dawn, before walkers start disturbing the hill.

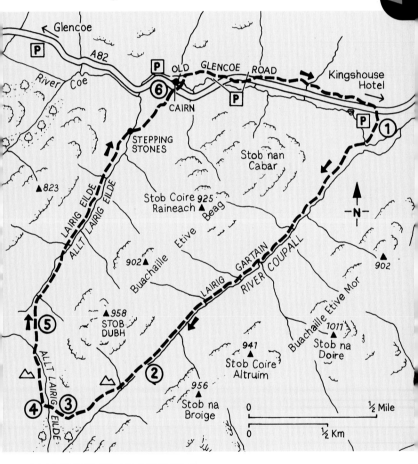

Walk 47 **Directions**

① A signpost to Glen Etive, at the edge of the car park, marks the start of the path into **Lairig Gartain**. The path is clear, but very boggy in

places. It heads up-valley with the **River Coupall** down on the left. Gradually it draws closer to the river, but does not cross it. A large cairn marks the top of the path, which is slightly to the right of the lowest point of the pass.

Walk 47

② The descending path is steeper, over boggy grass with a new stream forming on its left. After ½ mile (800m), a small path branches off left towards a waterfall below, but beware, as it's a wrong turning leading down to the roadside at Glen Etive, so stay on the main, higher path. This slants along the right-hand wall of the valley, getting ever higher above the stream. Eventually it emerges on to the steep south ridge of **Stob Dubh**.

③ Here a path runs down to a gate in a deer fence, but there's no need to go any further downhill. Follow a faint path above the deer fence, descending to cross the **Allt Lairig Eilde**. If the stream is too full to cross, you can return and go down through the deer fence to a wider but shallower crossing, 200yds (183m) downstream. Alternatively, you can head up on a small path to right of the stream, hoping to find a safer crossing higher up. Having crossed the stream, follow

the fence up to a gate at its corner. Turn up a wide path that rises out of **Glen Etive**.

④ The path ascends to the left of the stream, passing several waterfalls. Eventually it crosses the stream, now very much smaller, then continues straight ahead, crossing the col well to the right of its lowest point. A large cairn marks the top of the path.

⑤ The new, descending stream is also, confusingly, the **Allt Lairig Eilde**. The path crosses it by a wide, shallow ford and goes down its left bank. A mile (1.6km) further on, the path recrosses, using large boulders as stepping stones. It runs down to join the **A82** near the cairn that marks the entry into **Glen Coe**.

⑥ Cross the road, and the river beyond, to join the old Glencoe road at an arched culvert. Turn right along the firm track, which soon rejoins the new road, then cross diagonally, on to a damp path. This runs to the right of the new road, then recrosses. It soon rejoins the **A82** opposite the beginning of the walk.

Loch an Eilein's Castle and Ord Ban

The castle on the island in the loch is the heart of Rothiemurchus Forest.

•DISTANCE•	4¼ miles (6.8km)
•MINIMUM TIME•	1hr 45min
•ASCENT / GRADIENT•	100ft (30m)
•LEVEL OF DIFFICULTY•	
•PATHS•	Wide smooth paths, optional steep hill with high ladder stile
•LANDSCAPE•	Ancient pine forest around loch
•SUGGESTED MAP•	aqua3 OS Explorer 403 Cairn Gorm & Aviemore
•START / FINISH•	Grid reference: NH 897084
•DOG FRIENDLINESS•	On leads on Rothiemurchus Estate
•PARKING•	Estate car park near Loch an Eilein
•PUBLIC TOILETS•	Visitor centre

BACKGROUND TO THE WALK

An island castle, surrounded by ancient pines, and the mountains rising behind – you hardly have to bother with the rest of Scotland, Loch an Eilein has it all.

Castle for Cattle Thieves

Loch an Eilein Castle was built by John Comyn II, known as the Red Comyn, in the 13th century. It guards the strategic cattle-stealing route, the Rathad nam Meirleach, which runs along the shore of the loch. Locals used to keep a cow tied to a tree in hope that the raiders would take that and leave the rest alone. The three murderers of a Macintosh chieftain were imprisoned in chains here for seven years, before being executed in 1531. The castle was most recently fought over in 1690. Grizzel Mhor (Big Grizelda), the chieftain's wife, held it for Clan Grant against the King in 1690. There is said to be an underwater zig-zag causeway leading out to the island.

Life in the Pines

Walk quietly with binoculars and you may see some of the unique birdlife of the forest. The crested tit resembles the more familiar coal tit, with brown body and striped head, but with the Mohican hair-style effect of its crest. It nests in holes in old, rotten trees, so will only be found in wild forest. The Scottish crossbill, found only in Scotland, has a parrot-like beak, adapted for cracking open pine cones. The capercaillie is the large grouse of the forest and its name means 'horse of the woods'. The male challenges and intimidates other males with a noise like the clip-clop of hooves, or like a wine-bottle being opened. Your only real chance of seeing it in the wild is at dawn, in spring, at the RSPB reserve at Loch Garten (better known for its ospreys).

Osprey Island

Ospreys used to nest in the castle ruins. An egg collector once swam across wearing nothing but his cap, which he used to bring back his plunder. Ospreys are back in the Cairngorms,

Walk 48

and though they won't return to this over-public island, you might see them elsewhere plunging feet-first as they strike for a trout. Try the trout farm at Inverdruie, on the edge of Aviemore. Sadly, the egg-collectors are back as well. In 2000, a man in Leicester was caught with three stolen osprey eggs.

Romantic Setting

In the romantic novel *The Key above the Door* by Maurice Walsh (1926), the hero and heroine spend half the book gazing at each other from cottages on opposite sides of Loch an Eilein before accidentally getting shipwrecked on the island. More recently, Archie and Katrina, from the popular TV series *Monarch of the Glen*, enjoyed their own romantic encounter on the island.

Walk 48 Directions

① From the end of the car park at the beginning of the walk, a made-up path leads to the visitor centre. Turn left to cross the end of **Loch an Eilein**, then turn right on a smooth sandy track. The loch shore is near by on the right. There are small paths leading down to it if you wish to visit. Just past a red-roofed house, a deer fence runs across, with a gate.

② The track now becomes a wide, smooth path, which runs close to the loch side. After a bridge, the main track forks right to pass a bench backed by a flat boulder. The smaller path on the left leads high into the hills and through the famous pass of the **Lairig Ghru**, eventually to Braemar. After crossing a stream at a low concrete footbridge, the path bends right for 120yds (110m) to a junction. Just beyond is a footbridge with wooden handrails.

> ### WHAT TO LOOK FOR ⓘ
> At the foot of the loch, you walk across a low **loggers' dam**. Timber men used to release the water to carry the tree trunks down to the Spey. We usually think of the log-rafts of the great Canadian rivers, but the skill was carried there by Highlanders from Rothiemurchus.

③ To shorten the walk, cross this footbridge and continue along the main track, passing Point ④ in another 170yds (155m). For a longer walk, turn left before the footbridge on to a narrower path that will pass around **Loch Gamhna**. This second loch soon appears on your right-hand side. Where the path forks, keep right to pass along the loch side, across its head (rather boggy) and back along its further side, to rejoin the wider path around **Loch an Eilein**. Turn left here.

④ Continue around Loch an Eilein, with the water on your right, to a reedy corner of the loch and a bench. About 55yds (51m) further, the path turns sharply right, signposted 'footpath'. After a gate, turn right to the loch side and a **memorial** to Major General Brook Rice who drowned here while skating. Follow the shore to the point opposite the castle, then back up to the wide track above. A deer fence on the left leads back to the visitor centre.

⑤ From here, a stiff climb (around 500ft/152m) can be made on to the rocky little hill of **Ord Ban**, a superb viewpoint. Cross a ladder stile immediately to the right of the toilet block and follow the deer fence to the right for 150yds (137m), to a point behind the car park. Just behind one of the lowest birches on the slope, a small path zig-zags up the steep slope. It slants to the left to avoid crags, then crosses a small rock slab (take care if wet) and continues on to the summit. Descend by the same path.

> ### WHERE TO EAT AND DRINK ⓘ
> **Smiffy's Fish & Chips** at Aviemore is celebrated across Scotland by hungry hillwalkers and climbers. For even hungrier ones, **La Taverna** offers a pizza and salad 'eat as much as you can' buffet, as well as more formal Italian restaurant fare. You can find it at the south end of Aviemore, opposite the turn-off to Glenmore.

> ### WHILE YOU'RE THERE ⓘ
> Careful observers might see the wildcat, pine marten and capercaillie, but it's several centuries too late to spot the extinct wolf, bison and lynx. However, all these can be seen at the **Highland Wildlife Park** at Kincraig. It's an outpost of Edinburgh zoo, where all the Cairngorms' wildlife past and present is kept under fairly natural conditions.

Walk 49

Seeing Sea Eagles at Portree Bay

A coastal walk to a raised beach called the Bile, then returning by way of Ben Chracaig.

•DISTANCE•	2¾ miles (4.4km)
•MINIMUM TIME•	1hr 15min
•ASCENT / GRADIENT•	400ft (122m) ▲▲▲
•LEVEL OF DIFFICULTY•	🚶🚶 🚶🚶 🚶🚶
•PATHS•	Smooth, well-made paths, farm track, 3 stiles
•LANDSCAPE•	Views across Minch from wooded coast and hill above
•SUGGESTED MAP•	aqua3 OS Explorer 409 Raasay, Rona & Scalpay or 410 Skye – Portree & Bracadale
•START / FINISH•	Grid reference: NG 485436
•DOG FRIENDLINESS•	On leads through farmland, scoop poop on shore path
•PARKING•	Daytime-only parking on main A855 above Portree Harbour. Small parking area at slipway
•PUBLIC TOILETS•	Town centre

BACKGROUND TO THE WALK

While walking beside Portree Bay, keep at least one eye looking out to sea. You may spot what has been described as Britain's greatest conservation story – ever.

Sea Eagle Story

The last sea eagle in Scotland died on Skye in the early 1900s. Like all large raptors, it was shot at by shepherds and gamekeepers. An attempt to reintroduce them in 1959 was unsuccessful. In 1975, a secret RAF mission flew four young birds from Norway to the island of Rum. Over the next ten years, they were joined by 80 more. Today, about a dozen pairs are nesting, with a total population of around 100 spread up the western coast and the Hebrides.

In Gaelic it is called 'iolaire suil na greine' – the eagle with the sunlit eye – as its eye is a golden colour. In English it's also called the white-tailed eagle, the white-tailed fish eagle and the European sea eagle; it hasn't been back here long enough to finalise its name. Its nickname is the 'flying barn door' because it's so big, but it's not a heavy bird. Even with its 8ft (2.4m) wingspan, it weighs in at just 7lb (3kg). The sea eagle nests in cliffs. One nest, with an RSPB hide, is at Loch Frisa on Mull, another here at Portree. The Aros visitor centre has a closed-circuit TV camera trained on the nest, and the Portree fisherman have taken to throwing seafood to the birds outside the bay. The eagle feeds by snatching fish out of the sea – but even more spectacular is its mating display, when the two birds soar and cartwheel high above the water.

Was That An Eagle?

The first few eagles you think you see are almost certainly buzzards. When you see a real eagle, and even though you can't tell how far away it is, you'll know it for what it is. It's four times the size of a buzzard and its wingbeats are so slow and powerful. That's when it isn't gliding from one horizon to the other apparently without moving a feather. The sea eagle is even bigger than the golden one, and has a white tail – but so does a young golden eagle. But if the eagle is flying over the sea, and specially if it's over the sea at Portree, then it's a sea eagle.

Naturalists believed that the bird's main problem would be the golden eagle, which during the years of extinction has taken over the nest sites. But sadly, the real enemy is still humans. In 2000, and despite a 24-hour guard, thieves took the two eggs from the Mull pair.

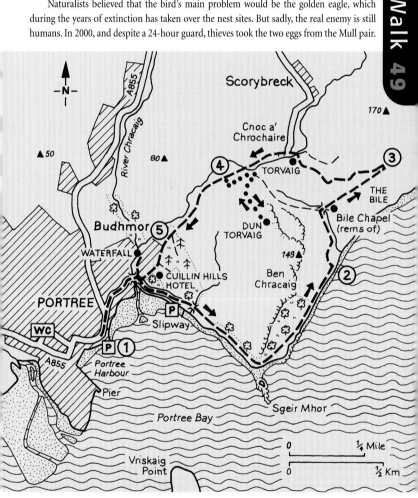

Walk 49 **Directions**

① Turn off the main **A855** on a lane signed 'Budh Mor', down to the shoreline and continue to a small parking area. A tarred path continues along the shore. After a footbridge, it passes under hazels which show the ground-branching

habit of bushes formerly coppiced, cut back every seven years for firewood. The path then rounds the headland to reach the edge of a level green field called **the Bile**.

② A wall runs up the edge of the Bile. Ignore a small gate, but turn left with the wall on your right. Just before the field corner you pass a

Walk 49

large fuchsia bush, spectacular in mid-summer. About 25yds (23m) later the path forks. Turn right, crossing a small stream and the wall, to head along the top edge of the Bile. Turn right, down a fence, to a field gate. Cross the top of the next field on an old green path, to a stile at its corner. You will see a track just beyond.

WHERE TO EAT AND DRINK ℹ
The informal Well Plaid bar/restaurant is at the **Royal Hotel** above the harbour. On the pier itself is the **Lower Deck** seafood restaurant, with a chip shop for those in a hurry. Near the start of the walk is the **Cuillin Hills Hotel**, a former MacDonald hunting lodge, now serving good bar meals.

③ Turn sharp left, up the track. At the top it passes through two gates to reach a stony road just to right of **Torvaig**. Turn left past the house and cross the foot of a tarred road into a gently descending track. It runs down between two large corrugated sheds and through to a gate with a stile.

④ The grassy path ahead leads down into Portree, but you can take a short, rather rough, diversion to **Dun Torvaig** (an ancient fortified hilltop) above. For the dun, turn left along the fence, and left again on a well-made path above. It leads to a kissing gate above the two sheds. Turn sharp right along the fence for

a few steps, then bear left around the base of a small outcrop and head straight up on a tiny path to the dun. Remnants of dry-stone walling can be seen around the summit. Return to the gravel path, passing above Point ④ to join the wall on the right. The path leads down under goat willows into a wood where it splits; stay close to the wall.

⑤ At the first houses (**The Parks Bungalow 5**), keep downhill on a tarred street. On the left is the entrance to the **Cuillin Hills Hotel**. A few steps later, fork right on to a stony path. At the shore road, turn right across a stream and at once right again on a path that runs up for 60yds (55m) to a craggy little waterfall. Return to the shore road and turn right to the walk start.

WHAT TO LOOK FOR ℹ
The strangely level meadow called the Bile is a **raised beach** that formed during the ice age. As the ice melted, the sea level rose, but at the same time, the land rose much further as the weight of overlying ice was removed. The result is that this former beach is now 100ft (30m) above the sea.

WHILE YOU'RE THERE ℹ
The **Aros Experience**, just south of Portree, has the RSPB's closed circuit TV link with the sea-eagle nest. Nest action is between April and July (the young hatch in April). The centre also has an exhibition and audio-visual centre dedicated to the people of Skye, including Bonnie Prince Charlie. Outside there are some short forest walks.

Flowerdale Falls

Porpoise-watching along the Gairloch shore, then up a rocky valley.

•DISTANCE•	5¼ miles (8.4km)
•MINIMUM TIME•	2hrs 45min
•ASCENT / GRADIENT•	800ft (244m) ▲ ▲ ▲
•LEVEL OF DIFFICULTY•	🚶 🚶 🚶
•PATHS•	Tracks and smooth paths, mostly waymarked, no stiles
•LANDSCAPE•	Gentle river valley and rocky coast
•SUGGESTED MAP•	aqua3 OS Explorer 433 Torridon – Beinn Eighe & Liathach or 434 Gairloch & Loch Ewe
•START / FINISH•	Grid reference: NG 807756
•DOG FRIENDLINESS•	On lead past Flowerdale House (as signs indicate)
•PARKING•	Beach car park, southern end of Gairloch
•PUBLIC TOILETS•	Walk start and Charlestown pier

BACKGROUND TO THE WALK

On a calm day in 1809, three fisherman drowned in Loch Ewe when their small boat was attacked and sunk by a whale. These Hebridean waters are among the best in Europe for cetaceans (whales, dolphins and porpoises). The Gulf Stream brings warm, plankton-rich water and the swirling currents around the islands bring nutrients to the surface. The plankton flourish; the fish eat the plankton; the whales and dolphins eat the fish.

Porpoise or Dolphin?

The strongest currents are at headlands and narrow sea passages, so these are good places to look for marine wildlife. Calm days are best, and early morning best of all when looking west, as the low sunlight shines off their wet backs. On most summer days, either the harbour porpoise or common dolphin – or possibly both – can be seen, given a little patience, in Loch Gairloch.

But which is which? At 6ft (2m) or less, the porpoise is smaller. It has a short, stubby fin compared with the dolphin's more elegant one. Harbour porpoises are normally shy, but the ones at Gairloch are untypically friendly, often approaching boats. Endangered in the world as a whole, the ones at Gairloch are doing well and a Special Area of Conservation has been proposed for them here.

What the Future Holds

The whaling industry in Scotland ended in 1951, but serious threats remain. Dolphins and porpoises are accidentally caught in fishing nets and floating plastic rope and old nets are another danger. Pollution from agriculture and forestry releases heavy metals and pesticides into the ocean. Fish farming is also probably damaging the dolphins. More fish sewage than human sewage goes into the Hebridean seas, all of it untreated, and anti-fouling paint on fish farms contributes more chemical pollutants, pesticides and antibiotics.

Cetaceans use sound signals through the water for finding fish, as well as for communication. Human noise interference comes from ships, dredging nets, seismic oil exploration and seal scammers – underwater beepers fitted to fish farms.

We don't know how well the dolphins and porpoises are doing. The growth of the whale-spotting industry means that we are just starting to discover how the populations are growing or declining. Marine tourism is now a £9 million concern with 400 jobs. By going on one of these trips, you will probably become a dolphin enthusiast, but also contribute to crucial research. A responsible boatman will not pursue the animals or steer into the middle of a group, but move quietly and wait for the dolphins to approach the boat.

Walk 50 **Directions**

① Cross the road and head up to the right of the **cemetery**. Turn left at its corner, going into trees to a

track above. Turn right until a footbridge leads on to a wide path that runs downhill. With a wall corner ahead, turn right (signed 'Flowerdale Waterfall'). A track runs down to a tarred driveway.

Walk 50

② Turn left to pass **Flowerdale House**. The way is marked with red-topped poles. The track passes to the left of a lovely old barn and turns right at another sign for the waterfall to pass **Flowerdale Mains**. In about ¼ mile (400m) you pass a concrete bridge on the right.

③ Follow the main path ahead, still to the left of the stream to reach a footbridge built by the Royal Engineers, just before you get to **Flowerdale Waterfall**.

WHAT TO LOOK FOR ⓘ

The **buzzard** often soars above the glen on wide, rounded wings and fanned tail. Like the much smaller kestrel, it can hover on fluttering wings while examining the ground below. In spring you may hear its mewing cry, not unlike a kitten. Once you're familiar with the buzzard, you'll have no trouble identifying the **golden eagle**, which looks similar but is three or four times the size.

④ The path leads up past the waterfall to cross a footbridge just above. It runs up into a pine clump, then turns back down the valley. After another footbridge it joins a rough track, which itself meets a forest road beside Point ③. Turn left, away from the concrete bridge, through felled forest that's being allowed to regenerate naturally with at least five separate species (birch, alder, pine, willow and rowan).

WHILE YOU'RE THERE ⓘ

The **Gairloch Marine Life Centre** has a display on cetaceans, seals and seabirds. It runs two-hour cruises on the *Starquest*, where you'll almost certainly see porpoises and seals, and possibly dolphins and minke whales. Every trip contributes to scientific knowledge of the wildlife populations. Cruises depend on the weather and are often fully booked.

⑤ Look out for a blue-topped pole marking a path on the right with a footbridge. It leads on through meadowland and bracken with blue waymarker poles. The path bends right at an old fence cornerpost and goes down through encroaching bracken and birch to pass above and to the left of an enclosed field. Turn right under two large oak trees and cross a small stream to an earth track.

⑥ Turn left for a few steps, until a small bracken path runs up to the right past a waymarked power pole. The path bends left under oaks, then drops to rejoin the earth track. This soon meets a larger track, which is the old road from Loch Maree to Gairloch. Turn right along this, through a couple of gates, to reach the **Old Inn** at Charlestown.

WHERE TO EAT AND DRINK ⓘ

The **Old Inn**, beside the former bridge over the Abhainn Ghlas in Charlestown, offers live music, fresh local seafood (including a cook-what-you-catch service), a barbecue grill and outdoor tables. Dogs are allowed in the outdoor section. The one thing it lacks, due to intervening buildings, is a sea view. **Flowerdale Mains farm** serves teas and snacks in summer.

⑦ Cross the old bridge, and the main road, to the pier. Turn right at a sign for Gairloch Chandlery, to find a tarmac path signposted for the beach. This passes to the left of a pinewood, then turns right into the trees. It bends left and emerges to run along the spine of a small headland. Just before being carried out to sea it turns sharp right, and crosses above a rocky bay to the fort (**An Dun**). A duckboard path runs along the back of the beach, then turns right to the car park.

Acknowledgements

Front cover: Red stag in Glengoulandie Deer Park, AA World Travel Library/H Williams